Why Does My Mother's Day Potted Plant Always Die?

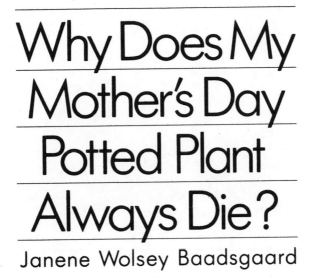

Why Does My Mother's Day Potted Plant Always Die?

Janene Wolsey Baadsgaard

Deseret Book Company
Salt Lake City, Utah

First printing March 1988
Second printing July 1988

Library of Congress Cataloging-in-Publication Data

Baadsgaard, Janene Wolsey
    Why does my Mother's Day potted plant always die? / by
Janene Wolsey Baadsgaard.
        p.   cm.
        Includes index.
        ISBN 0-87579-144-1 : $9.95
        1. Motherhood—United States—Anecdotes, facetiae, satire, etc.
2. Mothers—United States—Anecdotes, facetiae, satire, etc.
3. Child rearing—United States—Anecdotes, facetiae, satire, etc.
I. Title.
HQ759.B215   1988
306.8'743—dc19   88-482
                                                          CIP

For Ross

Contents

CONTENTS

Introduction

Growing up in the middle of eight girls, I rarely addressed my sisters by name. I called one sister "Leave my things alone," another, "It's your turn to do the dishes," and still another, "You always use all the hot water."

Being a sister in my house was not so much a choice as a fact. It was something I would have avoided at times. But there were other times . . . times like my graduation night.

Diane and Mary, my two older sisters, had tried for years to transform me. They were both great at applying makeup, styling hair, and selecting fashionable clothes. They had boyfriends, went to dances and parties, and spent hours sunbathing in the backyard.

I was their embarrassing younger sister. I thought sunbathing was a fancy name for wasting a whole afternoon in the lounge chair sweating. Nylons made my legs itch and hair spray made the fuzzies in my nose stiff. Even when we were small children and played with paper dolls together, Diane and Mary were left with gaping mouths when I freed all my paper ladies from their glamorous, frozen poses. I regularly cut my paper dolls up to their navels so they could run.

It had been a valiant effort. These two older sisters had worked on me for eighteen years without much success.

Then came the early evening before my high school seminary graduation. I was downstairs in my bedroom looking through the closet for something nice to wear. On rare occasions I could be persuaded to take a bath and wear a dress. This was a rare occasion. I was going to be one of the speakers, and I wanted to look nice.

My closet was full of hand-me-downs from Diane and Mary. It had never bothered me until now. It was the end of the month, and the family paycheck hadn't been able to stretch quite far enough to include a new graduation dress for me.

I understood. Being raised in the middle of many children teaches one to understand a lot of things. But sometimes it doesn't take away the wishing. I was wishing I had a new dress to wear.

I selected a nice navy blue dress with a white lace collar and pearl buttons. It had been Mary's graduation dress two years ago and it would just have to do. I zipped up the dress and slipped on a pair of dressy black shoes. They were run over on the heel and fit the foot form of their previous owner, my older sister Diane. They would have to do, too.

I grabbed my speech and walked upstairs, ready to leave. When I got to the head of the stairs, I saw Diane and Mary standing together smiling. Each of them was holding a package wrapped with fancy paper and shiny bows like the expensive department stores used.

Most of our family presents were wrapped in paper and bows my mom had saved from previous birthdays and holidays. We were taught to unwrap carefully.

I took the presents from my sisters as they put their arms around me and kissed me on both cheeks. The first present was large and rectangular. I opened the gift slowly, being careful not to rip the fancy wrapping paper under the tape. When I lifted the lid and folded back the tissue paper, a bright yellow chiffon dress with folded pleats on the front yoke shone out with the same warmth as the smiles on my sisters' faces.

The next box held a pair of bright yellow shoes, an exact match, with round toes and ties. A middle child in a large family never gets a pair of bright yellow shoes. It's just not practical.

"Run downstairs and put them on," Diane said.

"Hurry, or you'll be late," Mary added.

I ran back downstairs and tried on my new outfit. As I slipped the dress over my head and tied the laces on the shoes, I was magically transformed. I felt beautiful.

Diane was at that time a newlywed struggling to pay a huge medical debt incurred with her first baby daughter, who had died of a heart defect. Mary was a college student working hard to earn her tuition. The money to buy that dress and shoes did not come easily, and I knew it.

When I stood up to give my speech that night, I was clothed in something more than new clothes. It wasn't so much the dress and shoes as it was the whole shared history before — midnight talks on the double bed, the letter tucked under my pillow after I lost the election, crowded bathrooms, and tied-up telephones.

We were sisters.

It has been years since that night. My sisters and I have now all experienced mothering. We have not all physically borne children of our own, but we have all endured and delighted in the labor that children bring.

We have all found that our greatest frustrations and joys spring from working with children, whether it be in the home, classroom, office, hospital, or neighborhood. It is this shared history of mothering that gave birth to this book.

There is no typical mother, thank goodness. But the panic and pleasure we all experience as we work with children gives us a shared history.

We are all sisters.

So sit back, take off your girdle, prop up your feet, and enjoy this journey through seasons we all share.

SPRING

Ahhh, spring.

Summer and winter stretch into months of hot and cold. But spring sneaks up on us, then poof! it's gone.

Babies are like that. They sneak up on you before you're ready to let go of your own childhood, then, poof—they're gone.

I remember lying on the delivery table with my first child. Up until this point, I thought it would be "fun" having kids. After a particularly difficult contraction, I looked up at my doctor and insisted, "I don't want to do this anymore."

"Ready or not," he replied.

If This Is the Best Time, I Don't Want to Be Around for the Worst

"This is the best time of your life!" my elderly neighbor chuckled as I threw down the hose and raced to rescue my one-year-old, who was tumbling down the steps of our new home.

If one more person says that to me, I'm going to scream! I thought as I tried to comfort my crying baby and watched my two-year-old from the corner of one eye. I was four months pregnant with our third child and trying to keep our newly seeded lawn wet in hundred-degree weather.

"Your lawn's coming along fine," my elderly neighbor smiled as she walked toward me. Her face was dry and scented with cake powder. She seemed so calm and composed. I was perspiring and trembling with frustration.

"How can you say that?" I asked. "I can't even see any grass for all those weeds. Sometimes I think that's all I ever do — water the weeds."

"Don't worry about the lawn," advised my neighbor. "You'll see. Pretty soon all this watering will pay off, and your grass will crowd out all those weeds. All new lawns are like this. But things will change." She waved as she walked back toward her house. "This is the best time of your life, dear."

Well, if this is the best, I thought, *I don't want to be around for the worst.*

I had decided older folks just didn't appreciate what they had. They could get up whenever they wanted. They had time to immerse themselves in music, literature, art — everything I didn't have time for.

Eating one meal without wanting to bring in the garden hose to wash down the kitchen and kids would have been the high point of my day. It seemed as though all I ever did was wash diapers, faces, walls, floors, clothes, or dishes. My hands looked like they hadn't been out of water in years. In the evenings, after the children were safely tucked in bed, I usually tried to fit in some writing, art, or music — but, more often than not, something else needed washing again.

Then, one morning, a concerned trip to the doctor brought warnings of a possible miscarriage and instructions for bed rest. The children were packed up and taken to my mother's. Suddenly I had all the time I longed for and all the bed rest I wanted. It was wonderful!

But as the days wore on, something strange happened. I started missing my water-dimpled hands. This "no-work-to-do" business was getting old in a hurry.

A week later, I was still resting and the miscarriage still threatened. Late one night, contractions began. My husband carried me to the car, and we drove to the hospital. Lying with my head in my husband's lap, I looked out the window into the black sky.

Later, at the hospital, the doctor advised me to be philosophic about the whole thing. "After all," he explained, "most women have a spontaneous abortion or two during their childbearing years."

I wanted to kick him in the teeth. The loss I felt was overpowering. My husband sat quietly at my side, his eyes red and tired.

Days later, at home, I sat outside on the porch with my two small daughters. I noticed that the lawn, after weeks of my absence, had really changed, just as my elderly

4

neighbor had predicted. The small, tender green seedlings were growing into mature blades of grass. All my watering had paid off.

It occurred to me that perhaps all the work involved in caring for a young family was like our newly seeded lawn. It seems to be all work and water at first — and it's hard to see the tender seedlings beneath the weeds.

I knew then that if I didn't stop and look, I would miss something important. I would miss the joy in my children's growing. In time they, like the lawn, would not require my constant care. And the time would have passed all too quickly.

Perhaps, unlike my neighbor had suggested, this was not the best time of life. In fact, it might be no better or worse than any other time. But I would have this time only once — and if I missed the joy of growing in everything around me or within myself, I would truly miss it all.

Church Time

I know why the men in our church have so many meetings. It's so they won't have to go home and help get the kids ready for church.

Most Mormon moms have the glorious opportunity of orchestrating the frantic race to get to church on time. And most church schedules are arranged so that mothers of young children develop early ulcers.

If you're lucky enough to get the early schedule, you have to get up with the chickens and fly. You drag your sleepy-eyed children out of bed and try to get them to hurry. (By the way, children have no idea what *hurry* means.) You can always tell which children have the early schedule at church. Their hair looks like someone took an eggbeater to it, then sprayed it with Elmer's Glue.

If you get the middle schedule, you spend your time trying to decide if you should feed the kids lunch at 10:00 A.M. so you can make it to church at 11:00, or whether to wait until you get home at 2:00. Of course, the first alternative means the kids won't eat because they're not hungry, and the latter alternative means your young children will turn into raving monsters during sacrament meeting.

If you get the late schedule, forget about naps. You get to shake your child awake, then drag this delightful companion with you to church and spend three hours keeping him quiet. Of course, no self-respecting baby would be caught dead falling asleep at church. That would make it too easy for Mom.

Once you know when your meeting is supposed to start,

your next challenge is to get there. Why do mothers with young children look as if they've just been through a war when they walk through the doors of the chapel?

They have.

The other day, I hurriedly tried to get my three-year-old ready for church on time. I still had the other two children to get ready and only five minutes to do it in.

My three-year-old sat leisurely down by her shoe box, calmly measuring the pros and cons of two pairs of dressy shoes.

"What's the matter with you?" I said impatiently. "Hurry up!"

She didn't seem to listen to me as she slowly rubbed her small index finger over the toe of each shoe.

"These are too slickery," she said, "but these make my feet too squished." Then she noticed a toy truck next to her on the floor. She picked it up and made a vroom sound as she rolled the truck up and down the shoe box.

"Don't you know how to hurry?" I asked, my voice raising noticeably in volume.

My three-year-old looked at me, puzzled. She tried to stand up, but tripped over her shoes.

"We're going to be late! We're going to be late!" I chanted. "If you don't hurry up, we're going to be late!"

My three-year-old wrinkled her nose and peered at me, fascinated with my animated facial gestures and agitated tone of voice. Then she put her arms up in the air and stretched leisurely as she yawned.

I quickly walked over to her, picked her up off the floor, and sat her down briskly on the bed next to me. At that point, my four-year-old ran into the bedroom, her face covered with raspberry jam, and announced cheerfully, "I think the baby did something suspicious in his pants, Mom. He sure is stinky."

My three-year-old put her arm around me as I quickly finished buckling her shoes and said, "Mom, what's *hurry* mean?"

Getting to church is only part of the problem. Keeping the kids quiet once you get there is another part.

Every ward or branch has one Polly Perfection who sews the family look-alike dresses and bow ties. They sit together on the front row, of all places, looking like an *Ensign* magazine cover. None of her children have coloring books, Cheerios, or quiet books. Her baby doesn't stomp Dinky Doughnut presweetened cereal into the carpet for the janitor to get mad about. Her baby sits up straight on her lap and listens to the speakers . . . even on High Council Sunday.

I am, of course, the mother standing up in the overflow section jiggling my baby up and down like a hot potato.

I guess I must have done something wrong in the pre-existence, the punishment for which was the curse of a buzzer bottom. As long as I stand up, my baby is fine. But just let me try to sit down and: "WAAAAAAA!" I think it works something like those dog whistles that have a high frequency sound that humans can't hear, but it sends dogs wild.

When my baby starts to fuss at the quietest moment of the service, I pick her up and try to soothe her. It doesn't work. I'm sitting on the buzzer, you see. So I get up and walk to the back of the church.

Soon, baby is sleeping soundly on my shoulder, even snoring. Slowly I edge myself back up to our bench and slowly, ever so slowly, I lower myself back into the seat. But as soon as I touch bottom . . . "WAAAAAAA!"

I wish someone would tell me how to unplug the thing.

Like Digging for Treasure

Life with children is like a career in archaeology. It sounds romantic and idealistic before you try it yourself. In reality, both require a little lunacy and a great deal of dirt under the fingernails.

So why do so many women opt for a life with kids? We're treasure hunters — that's why.

I approached my first experience on an archaeological dig much like I did my first experience with motherhood. I believed the rewards would be immediate and the work minimal.

I traveled halfway around the globe to a site in Israel for my first real dip into the world of eternal dirt. No one had ever leveled with me about archaeology work. I was in for a bit of a shock.

No one ever leveled with me about becoming a mother either, least of all the doctors and nurses. They put me flat on my back, proceeded with enemas, stuck me with needles, hooked me to machines, strapped my legs and arms down, then flashed bright lights in my eyes. All this and labor besides, and they still insisted that motherhood would be painless if I would just learn how to "breathe correctly."

That first morning at the dig (excavation) found me enthusiastic and ready for my first big discovery. I knew in a second I could unearth some important treasure. But when I dug the dirt away, I found more dirt. After I hauled that away in the wheelbarrow, I found more dirt.

My introduction to motherhood was like that. After I changed one diaper, there was another. After I fed the baby, she was hungry again. After I cleaned the house, it got dirty again. After I fixed a meal, it was time for the next one.

Minutes, hours, days, and weeks went by, and I hadn't made my amazing discovery at the dig. I was beginning to get depressed.

Minutes, hours, and sleepless nights went by with my newborn. After continually feeding one end of the little darling and cleaning up the other end, I was beginning to get depressed.

But time passed, and I survived.

The summer at the dig was over, and it was time to go home. I took a good look at myself. I had lost twenty pounds, was sunburned and insect-bitten, and had chronic diarrhea, blisters on my hands and feet, aching muscles, and a family of flies that circled around my head. There was a salt ring on my backside and a permanent layer of grit on my skin. Yet I was ready to cash in another life's savings and do the whole thing again.

After the first few weeks with my newborn daughter, I took a look at myself. My baggy stomach muscles were still hanging around my knees. I had a permanent spit-up stain on my shoulder, diaper-pin holes in all my fingers, bug eyes, uncombed hair, and I still had to sit on the doughnut pillow they gave me at the hospital. Yet after a year or so, I cashed in our life's savings and did the whole thing over again.

You see, it wasn't the grit, sun, and sore muscles that brought me so much satisfaction at the dig. It wasn't the spit-up and dirty diapers that brought me so much satisfaction with my child. It was and is the constant anticipation of finding treasure underneath what other people call work.

I didn't find a major archaeological treasure at the dig. But while I was getting tired and dirty digging up an ancient kitchen, I suddenly realized families through the ages haven't changed a great deal. I discovered that although my ancient predecessor had lived in a different time, she had loved, given birth, and yelled at her kids to close the door behind them. Now, I couldn't put that in a museum, but it was enough for me.

It is that same constant anticipation of finding treasure that sustains mothers everywhere today. Complete with mops and toilet plungers, mothers are the ultimate lifetime volunteers. Somewhere between the kitchen sink and the diaper pail, mothers are daily discovering something beneath all that mess.

Mothers everywhere dig through large mounds of accumulated childish clutter day after day. But there are times when we find a giggling toddler under all that mess, begging to be tickled, begging to be discovered, begging to be enjoyed.

We may not be able to put that in a museum, but it's more than enough for us.

Where Do Babies
Come From,
Mother Dear?

I write a column for the *Deseret News* on family life. One week I asked my readers for ideas on how to reduce the costs involved in having children.

One response I received offered a rather blunt suggestion. The unsigned note read, "Try birth control pills, abstinence. You don't need to be so self-indulgent."

Well . . . I used to be naive enough to believe that kind of propaganda myself. But since I've become a parent, I've had my eyes opened to the real "facts of life."

The problem with this reader's fact-oriented advice is that it fails to tell the real truth about how babies get here to start with. Babies aren't caused by . . . well, you know. If it were as simple as that, then everybody who wanted a baby would have one and those who didn't want one would never have any surprises.

There are far more reliable rules for contraception than this sincere but misinformed reader had to offer. If you want to be sure you don't get in a delicate condition,

1. announce to your parents, in-laws, friends, neighbors, co-workers, and ward or branch members that you and your husband are going to start your family now.

2. spend your savings redecorating your study into a nursery.

3. promise your daughter a baby sister for Christmas.

4. buy a bigger house.

5. quit your well-paying job after announcing to the world you are anxious for motherhood before it's too late.

6. graduate with straight A's in child development, obtain a master's degree in family relations and a Ph.D. in home management.

On the other hand, this is how babies are **really made.** Babies are made when

1. a wife finds a fascinating new career she loves, with unlimited possibilities for fame and fortune, and happily assures her new employer that she won't be having any more babies.

2. a husband and wife decide they have enough children and proceed to sell or give away all their baby clothes, furniture, and maternity clothes.

3. a doctor reassures a woman she doesn't need to worry any longer because she has "gone through the change."

4. a woman goes on a diet with her husband in which the first one to lose twenty pounds gets a whole new wardrobe.

5. the wife spends a seven-year clothing allowance on one dozen tight, form-fitting dresses.

6. a couple finally give up on the infertility doctors and decide to adopt triplets. This happy pair will promptly become pregnant with twins.

7. the couple forget to keep insurance policy payments current and find out they have been dropped from coverage, maternity benefits and all.

This same reader offered another unusual suggestion on how to reduce the costs of raising a family: "Institute a head tax for all the sexual gluttons who have more than the national average number of children."

As for the assumption that everyone with more than the national average of children is a sexual glutton, I have it from an experienced authority that it can work just the opposite way. The last time my husband and I felt even remotely gluttonous, Aubrey wanted a drink of water, Jordan fell off the top bunk bed, Joseph got his head stuck between the posts in the crib, Arianne had a nightmare, April got the stomach flu, and the baby wet the bed.

A Time to Laugh

During the parenting career of every mother, there are times when she feels downright sentimental toward her children.

There are other times when she doesn't.

There have been times, I must admit, when I have felt that gooey sentimentality that comes to a mother when her child accomplishes something of monumental proportions. Like the time I had been working for months to get my two-year-old to say that most precious of phrases. After a series of daily promptings, my little angel finally muttered that lovely phrase every mother waits to hear in her husband's presence: "I want Dada to change my pants."

I once heard of a professor in child development or parenting or something equally rigorous who had developed a unique way to help prepare naive students for the trials of the real thing—having kids of their own. He wanted his students to have some idea of what the constant responsibility, worry, and confinement of parenting were all about. So he had them carry raw eggs around with them all day, then report their feelings at the end of the day. "Confining, frustrating, hard, humorous, impossible, and difficult" were some of the comments he received.

These college kids thought they had it hard. Hah! Carrying an egg around for a day would be a piece of cake. Eggs don't have little legs that follow you into the bathroom. Eggs don't demand a drink of water at 2:00 A.M. Eggs can be broken only once, and the cleanup is quick and odorless. I do not believe children have the same merits.

My husband thought I was getting sentimental recently when he caught me crying as our baby took his first step. I wasn't crying because of time hurrying by unappreciated. I was crying because I realized that my once-prone infant was now able to reach into my makeup drawer.

The only people I know who are always sentimental about children are childless. All right, grandparents sometimes fall into this category too, but they are usually the ones who suffer from great amounts of memory loss.

Grandparents often tell young mothers that all they need is a sense of humor. But it's been twenty years since they had to pull the baby out of the garbage can or try to degrease the Vaseline-covered walls. Things like stick figures crayoned all over the new bedspread always seem a lot funnier when it's been twenty years since it happened to you.

My mother always laughs when I tell her about the baby getting into the kitchen cabinets. "That really brings back memories," she chuckles.

She can laugh. She didn't have to pick up the 2,364 pieces of elbow macaroni and sort them from the 8,000,000 grains of rice.

I seem to be the only one in my family that doesn't have a sense humor. Even my children laugh about things more than I do. They get especially amused whenever I say, "Don't do that!" or "Go clean it up!" or "Stop that!" They think it's funny to see the look on my face as I fish our newest four-pack of Charmin out of the toilet.

It's when I start laughing that everyone else's sense of humor disappears. When I laughed at my three-year-old for marching around the house with the strainer on her head and the flour sifter for a musical instrument, she indignantly stopped marching and said, "It's not funny, Mom."

I used to have a good sense of humor. Before I had children I used to laugh at my sister's daughter for walking around with her finger up her nose. My sister didn't laugh. She simply said, "You just wait."

Now my little boy walks around with his finger up his nose. It doesn't seem so funny anymore.

Last night, I walked into my children's bedroom. They should have been asleep long ago, but they were jumping up and down on the beds using their pillows for horses. When they saw me in the doorway, they stopped bouncing and looked at me fearfully, awaiting the reprimand.

I scowled at them for a moment and then blurted out, "You kids shouldn't be . . . " Then I thought back a few years, to when I used to jump on my bed using my pillow for a horse.

My daughters were silent, still waiting for me to complete my lecture. A smile crept across my face as I walked over, picked up a pillow, and started jumping up and down on their bed. At first my daughters were shocked, then they joined in the spontaneous rodeo.

You know, bouncing on the bed is still as much fun as it used to be.

The Hair Scare

When the doctor cut the cord and placed my first baby girl on my stomach, I remember she looked like she had lots of dark, curly hair. But each time the nurses bathed her and brought her to me, her hair looked a little lighter and thinner.

By the time she was six weeks old, my daughter's hairline resembled her grandpa's. She had plenty of hair in the back, but she was bald on the top and sides. She also developed infant acne just in time for her ward debut at her blessing. No one warned me about this.

When my second daughter, Aubrey, was born, she had just the opposite problem. Her hairline joined her eyebrows. She even had dark, downy hair on her back and shoulders.

When my son Jordan was born, I thought I had the problem solved. His hairline was where a hairline ought to be, near the top of the forehead. The only problem was that his hair stood straight up. No matter how much I brushed or plastered it down, in a few minutes it was standing straight up all over again. He looked like a dandelion gone to seed.

I figured if I would be patient, his hair would grow long enough that the sheer weight of it would force it to lay down on his head. No such luck. His hair grew at least a foot long, and it still looked like I'd thrown him in the dryer without a static control sheet.

One of my friends has a baby girl who is still bald at two years old. This mother makes her daughter wear a hat whenever she goes out in public.

Another one of my friends has a baby with gobs of long, dark, curly hair. But do you think she knows how to appreciate it? No. She's always complaining about trying to keep the morning mush out of it.

Another of my friends tries to make her bald baby girl look more like a female by sticking a ribbon on her head with Karo syrup. Whenever the baby sweats, the bow slowly drifts until it ends up at the south pole.

Protruding Pregnancy

Why do women have to carry their unborn children in such an obvious place? When you're good and pregnant, no one ever notices your face anymore. They look straight at that protruding middle and address your belly button. I've known pregnant women who have been tempted to glue facial features onto their maternity tops and learn to be ventriloquists.

If you are going to speak to a mother-in-waiting, please look at her face and watch your language. Do not say, "Haven't you had your baby yet?" If an expectant mother has had her baby, she will be holding it in her arms.

Do not say, "My, haven't you blossomed." Flowers blossom; women don't.

Do not say, "Do you want a girl or a boy?" Most all human mothers want a girl or a boy. I've never met anyone who wanted a dog or a cat.

Do not say, "How are you feeling?" Pregnant women feel pregnant . . . twenty-four hours a day.

Do not say, "How much longer do you have?" Pregnant women are frequent calendar gazers. They would love to tell you exactly how much longer—down to the second, if they knew. But nature does funny things to due dates. If a pregnant woman says she has months to go, she'll probably have her baby that night. If she says she's going to have the baby that night, she probably has months to go.

Now, if you are wondering what *to* say, try these . . .

"Would you like my chair?"

"May I tie your shoes?"

"May I pick it up for you?"

"May I scrub your bathtub?"

Most obstetricians will gladly discuss weight gain, diet, and embryo growth with pregnant women. But they always leave out the really important stuff every pregnant woman should know. For instance, no doctor will ever tell you that your usually depressed belly button will suddenly become protruding.

Doctors get hung up on things like weight gain. Scales are the most important part of a professional intimidation plan for expectant mothers. This torture is inflicted on a very vulnerable portion of the female population every month. It is more commonly referred to as "weighing in."

I'll never forget the day I went to the obstetrician's office for my very first pregnant-lady visit. Boy, was I naive.

The first thing I noticed when I entered the doctor's office was a waiting room full of very nervous patients. I took a seat next to an obviously pregnant lady. I noticed she was nervously making checks on a list in front of her.

"Let's see now," she said. "Water pill . . . Check! Remove nail polish . . . Check! Remove all jewelry and shoes . . . Check! Haircut . . . Check!"

"What are you doing?" I asked.

"I'm just going over my list of precautions before I step on the scales," she replied. "I haven't eaten anything for two days."

"Don't you think that's a little rash?" I asked. "I mean, after all, you are pregnant, and you're supposed to gain a little, aren't you?"

"Boy, are you naive!" the woman on the other side of me said. "You don't know what sort of intimidation they put you through in there. Why, I've even considered having my appendix removed and my tonsils taken out before I step on one of those things. My dentist refused to take out my fillings. I'd hate to get in an accident on the way here. It's not that I'm wearing holey underwear; it's that

21

I'm not wearing any at all. Every little bit helps. I even check for lint in my belly button."

Suddenly I heard my name being called by a nurse. I left the waiting room with the farewell wishes of my new friends.

"Step on the scales," the nurse ordered, pointing to the scales in military fashion.

"Don't you want to prick my finger, or take my blood pressure, or operate first?" I asked, suddenly understanding my new friends in the waiting room.

The nurse shook her head and tapped her pen impatiently on the chart.

At this point I removed any article of clothing that was not absolutely necessary for modesty.

More pen tapping.

I stepped as lightly as possible on that giver of secrets, hardly breathing as that insensitive nurse continued to push the pound gauge up and up. I felt like slapping her hand.

"You have gained," the nurse said sternly.

"Well," I answered, trying to think of some kind of excuse, "I didn't want to tell anyone, but I think I'm pregnant."

"I've heard that one before," she replied. "It's to the examination room with you."

When I left the doctor's office that day, I asked the woman in the waiting room for her checklist.

There has got to be a more humane way to treat pregnant women. You can ask them to do almost anything else that is impossible: find their feet, fit in a booth, scrub a bathtub, or suck in. But please don't ask them to step on the scales.

Rules of Child Discipline

Most experts tell us as new parents that we should avoid saying no to our children. Instead, we should divert the child's attention to something positive. These rules of discipline don't always work for me.

When my eighteen-month-old climbed up on the stove, sat down on a burner, then turned the knob to high, it didn't even occur to me to say, "Oh, dear, your pants are on fire. Wouldn't you rather play with your blocks?"

When my two-year-old ran out in front of a cement truck that was going sixty miles an hour, my first reaction was *not* to say, "Wouldn't you rather play on the grass?"

Experts then inform me that I should be consistent. I should react the same way each time my child misbehaves. I have trouble with this rule also.

The first time my daughter redid my entire bedroom decor in Vaseline and wet toilet paper, I took the jar away and said, "No, dear. You must never do that again."

After I finished cleaning and went in the other room, she did the whole thing over again, only this time she also smeared the stuff over her entire body.

My "NO, NO!" was much louder this time, and I hid the Vaseline. When I put her in the bathtub, she looked like a floating bath oil ball.

Later that evening, she found another jar of Vaseline and repeated the whole procedure. I did not act consistent. I did not act sane. I screamed, threw all oil-based products and toilet paper in the garbage, and put my child in solitary crib confinement for an undetermined sentence.

The experts also tell us that we shouldn't make threats. Children tend to live in the present and don't remember them. But threats seem to be the only things that work well with my children.

I learned the fine art of threatening from my own mother. To this day, I have to wash my hands and rewash them after using the bathroom for fear I'll get worms. She also told us that our guardian angel went to sleep at midnight. Don't ask me what happens to people without guardian angels, but I never ever stayed out after midnight to find out.

Experts also tell us that lecturing a child is not useful. They tell us to be brief with our reprimands. I really don't think this rule should pertain to me. When I even start to lecture my children, they put their hands over their ears and shut their eyes. It is annoying, but I persist.

Whenever I get a really good lecture going, invariably my two-year-old will start laughing and try to imitate my expressions, inflections, and finger wagging. "You look funny when you're mad, Mommy," he interrupts. It's hard to concentrate under those circumstances, so the lecture usually ceases.

The experts also tell us to make sure our children know exactly what is expected of them. My children know what I expect of them. They just don't care.

Maybe I'll just forget what the experts say. After all, they assume that I act like an adult all the time just because I'm a mother. I think I'll just try to grow up with my children.

Having children hasn't made me an instant "adult." Since I started having children, my age seems to vary. Sometimes I feel like I'm ninety-six. This is most often at the 2:00 A.M. feeding. At other times, I feel like I'm barely two years old. So if my children can survive my adult adolescence, I think I can survive their childhood.

Flash-card Momma

It's tough being a new parent these days. You see, I've read all those books and articles by Ph.D.'s that tell me my child's capacities and his entire future achievements are fixed in the first few years of life.

Talk about scary! It didn't even occur to me to play classical music to influence the fetus still in my womb. I've never gotten around to using flash cards with my three-month-old. It seemed like a lot more fun to blow on her tummy and watch her laugh. I didn't know my one-year-old was supposed to be exposed to Picasso. He was always too busy drawing purple and green trucks all over the living room walls.

According to the experts, I am supposed to be helping my child reach his full potential, and here I am still working on teaching him to keep his feet off the dinner table. It's embarrassing.

I'm obviously not winning in our current generation's parenting race. My babies simply refuse to be superbabies. They dare spend the entire first few months of their lives lounging around and pooping.

Here I am having fun playing "This Little Pig Went to Market" with my three-year-old when I'm supposed to be listening to him play the violin before large audiences. It's depressing.

But there are times . . .

I remember one of those ordinary mornings. My husband was hurrying to eat his last bite of toast and jam before he left for work. Our six young children were laughing, chattering, munching, gulping, and spilling while I hurried about the kitchen buttering toast, pouring orange juice, and flipping eggs.

The morning sunlight from the east kitchen window streamed into the kitchen, illuminating each face. My husband started playing with the baby. Everything was, as usual, chaotic, but then suddenly wonderful.

As I looked at them, I was instantly overcome with how much I loved them. I could scarcely speak or move. It was a moment of intense happiness.

It didn't last long. My husband soon pecked me on the cheek and left. The baby spilled his Cheerios, the two-year-old and the four-year-old started fighting, and the six-year-old refused to clear his dishes.

But I had that moment, that sun-sparkling moment, and it could and would sustain me through the morning of missing socks and messy diapers.

Blessings and Blunders

I received a call the other day from a warm, friendly volunteer at my local hospital. She courteously called me by name and asked what insurance company I belonged to.

I have a hard enough time keeping my own children's names straight. My insurance company's name always eludes me. To stall for time while my computer tried to remember, I asked, "Why do you want to know?"

"Well," she said, "we like to get everything ready for you before you're admitted. It makes things run a little smoother."

I am one to try to help things run smoother if possible, but I had no plans to be admitted in the near future, so I said, "But I don't plan to be admitted anytime soon, unless I get hit by a cement truck or develop an instant kidney stone sometime today."

She laughed. "No, when you come in to have your baby."

"What baby?"

"Your baby . . . aren't you expecting soon?"

"Not unless you know something I don't."

"This really blows my mind," the volunteer said, flustered. "This is Janene Baadsgaard, isn't it?"

"Well, yes, but that doesn't necessarily mean . . . "

"I wonder why we have your name on the computer list."

"Maybe this is some kind of an omen," I answered.

She laughed.

I didn't laugh. You see, in the past eight years, I have been pregnant seven times. We lost one child, and have six living children.

During these years of continual tummy-expanding experiences, I have received more than my fair share of questions and comments such as:

"Why do you have so many children?"

"Pregnant again?"

"Having a large family today isn't fair to you as a total woman. It stifles your talents and obligates you with responsibilities."

"Having so many children so close together isn't fair to the children, because your attention must be so divided."

I've pondered these questions and comments many times over the years — especially when the doctor sent me to bed with premature labor with my last pregnancy. Six weeks of lying around twiddling thumbs can give a plump body plenty of time to think. And I've come up with what are a few personal answers for me.

People seem afraid of responsibility today, as if it were a dirty word, something to be avoided at all costs. One assumes great responsibilities when one decides to have a child. But maybe a greater responsibility is decreeing that a young life shall not be.

In the chaos, clutter, and commotion I call my home, I have often doubted my abilities to give each of my children everything he or she has needed. But over the years, I have discovered I have been able to give my children something much more lasting than a room of their own, lots of nice clothes, and my continual undivided attention. I have given them each other.

That constant thing called a brother or sister can't be divorced or lost in a bad financial venture. My children always have someone to fight with and someone to laugh with. They have someone to slug and someone to hug. They have someone they're not speaking to and someone to tell all their secrets to. They have someone to sit next to at family reunions and someone to disown.

No matter how many children parents have, their love is complete for each child. Love can't be divided up like a piece of pie. The capacity to love grows with each new addition to the family.

As for stifling my creativity and ability to develop as a total woman, my children have proven to be the catalyst as well as the subject of my career in writing.

Even though I have to share the bathroom and hot water with seven other people, and a new dress for Mom is an every-other-year event celebrated with a family fashion show and refreshments, I think there is such a thing as too much privacy and too many possessions.

Yes, my family takes up my space. Yes, it takes up my time. But it is is also my family that has given me everything to feel and something to say.

A Young Mother's Dream Should Never Come True

Someday, I keep telling myself, all my children will be in school. I will suddenly have six blessed hours all to myself. I've been dreaming for years of all the great stuff I would write when my children quit interrupting me.

But last night I had a nightmare. In my dream, I saw myself sitting down at a solid oak, roll-top desk with a golden pen in hand, instead of a damaged door atop two worn-out end tables, which is what I have now. Everything was ready for long, quiet hours of uninterrupted work. I put my pen to paper, but nothing happened.

I looked around for some kind of inspiration or distraction. But there were no three-year-olds walking around acting out cute little anecdotes. No one was fighting or screaming. I couldn't hear Cookie Monster, Big Bird, or Mister Rogers singing in the background. No one wanted a snack. No one wanted anything. It was enough to drive me nuts.

I saw myself get up from the desk in an attempt to find a little distraction. But as I walked through the house, there were no blocks or teething rings to pick up. There were no toddlers glued to my legs with every step I took. There wasn't even anybody to keep me company when I went to the bathroom.

Then I saw myself trying to make the bed. There was no one to sit on the blankets while I tried to pull them up. There was no one to throw pillows at me or bounce up and down on the bed when I was through.

I saw myself trying to wash the dishes, but there was no one to "help" me by dripping water from wet plates across the kitchen floor. There wasn't anyone to play submarine with me in the soapsuds.

Nobody begged me to read a story. Nobody needed a nose wiped or a shoe tied. Nobody asked for a peanut-butter cracker or whined to be rocked to sleep on my shoulder. Nobody wanted anything.

Every time I cleaned a room, it stayed clean. Every time I vacuumed, the carpet pile stayed up. Nobody jumped on my back and asked me for a horsie ride when I was down on my hands and knees wiping up the kitchen floor that nobody had spilled milk on.

I had to go back to my desk and work.

"What's the matter?" my husband asked me as he shook me awake.

"I've just had the most terrible nightmare," I told him.

Later that morning, I went for a walk with my pre-schoolers. We all got messy, dragged our coats in the dirt, and touched everything. At the lunch table, we all talked with our mouths full, bubbled in our milk, and wouldn't eat the liver.

I think I can wait for some dreams to come true.

SUMMER

Late one summer, I sat outside on the porch with my children huddled under the eaves as we watched a storm roll in. We felt the cool, gentle rain on our faces and watched the deep, rolling, gray clouds tumbling over one another, filling the troubled sky.

Soon the slow, uneven raindrops falling against us turned into rain-sheets swept across the sky by the gusting winds. We raced inside and watched the rest of the storm from our home's warm interior.

Later the rain slowed and gradually stopped. The sun in the western horizon broke through a small opening in the storm clouds. The sky became a panorama of changing colors. Deep ambers, brilliant golds, cool wet blues, and translucent whites filled the previously gray sky.

Sometimes my family life feels like a storm. Then time passes. The storm blows over.

I try to remember that storms come, but storms go.

Garden Daze

During the summer, green-thumb mothers get out the old hoe and put in a garden. All this provident living makes us sleep better at night—or does it?

Some small Mormon communities celebrate summer with Pioneer Day a few days before the really big celebration: Zucchini Days. Zucchini Days start innocently enough. Loyal gardeners with good pioneer ancestry get out early every year and start working the soil. They faithfully pay their fee so they can have irrigation water once a week, and they spend hours weeding their patch of backyard dirt.

Of course, no gardener worth his salt would forget to plant that famous vegetable, the honorable zucchini. Every gardener knows that even if all else fails, the zucchini will survive and produce en masse. Except he forgets just how much mass.

Each summer, he remembers. Then the frantic celebration begins.

Owning a zucchini plant is like owning a very fertile female cat. You are constantly getting little batches of babies.

At first, they are adorable and you love to tend and take care of them. Then when you turn your back, they are suddenly regenerated. You are constantly calling your neighbors, friends, and enemies to find someone, anyone, who will give a new home to your latest litter.

Check the cupboards in any Mormon Mama's kitchen and you'll find a whole file of zucchini recipes. You see, we wouldn't be caught dead wasting even one skinny green darling. Thanks to countless Relief Society homemaking demonstrations, we have mastered the art of dilled zucchini, zucchini marmalade, baked zucchini, zucchini casserole, zucchini boats, zucchini pie, zucchini omelets, french-fried zucchini, chocolate zucchini cake, wheat germ zucchini bread, cream of zucchini soup, zucchini salad, creamed zucchini, gelatin zucchini, scalloped zucchini, zucchini fritters, spicy pineapple zucchini bread, cinnamon zucchini bread, zucchini cheese puffs, soft zucchini cookies, stuffed zucchini, zucchini spaghetti sauce, whole wheat deep dish zucchini pizza, and zucchini with tomatoes and parmesan dumplings. We will go to great expense and put in long, grueling hours to put our green babies to good use.

Even if you have an excellent memory and don't plant this lovely squash plant, your neighbor will. You'll find anonymous brown bags left on your doorstep. You will, in short, become an orphanage for little green babies some parent can no longer provide for. There is simply no getting away from this celebration.

Zucchini has thirteen to sixteen calories per serving when boiled without butter. Zucchini is low in sodium and has appreciable amounts of vitamins A, C, and niacin. The only problem is that you have to dump a bucket of sugar or butter on this vegetable to taste it.

So why do we grow zucchini squash? Tradition. We want our children to go through what we endured as children.

But the rest of the garden — ahhhhhh . . .

There's nothing quite like a juicy red tomato minutes from the vine to your mouth. There is a certain magic about a striped watermelon just cracked down the ripe center, or golden delicious apples still wet with early morning dew. There's something non-cannable about a thick, red slice of tomato just waiting for a strip of bacon, a crunchy lettuce leaf, and two lightly browned pieces of toast spread with mayonnaise.

Most of the really great stuff can't be preserved. Good

fresh vegetables and fruits right at their peak of ripeness can't be told to wait a minute.

Children know how to enjoy a harvest. They eat it. They let Mom worry about having enough left over to bottle.

You have to grow a garden or live near someone who does to really get in on all this revelry. Dig a potato with your own two hands and you'll find gold of a different sort. Nurture a tree through infancy and puberty and you'll find yourself bearing fruit along with it.

It's quite a miracle, you know, all this wonderful food from a handful of seeds. There is hope in it all—hope you have to experience firsthand to understand.

There are seasons when we endure the cold and darkness, but there are times as fleeting as the late summer harvest when our efforts do bring fruit. We feel part of a pattern larger than ourselves, beyond our abilities. We feast, and the harvest is good for a time. Harvests in our lives are meant to be tasted today and savored, slowly savored.

When the frost does come, and it always does, and the leaves turn brittle and brown and fall from the trees, we can remember each delicious moment. That will almost be enough to get us through for another year until our harvest comes again. And it always does.

I don't think each of us receives one harvest only—an after-death sort of payment for services rendered. I think we all get a lifetime full of little harvests—those small miracles that stand out from the rest of life, when we are one with nature, each other, and ourselves.

So let the golden kernels linger on your tongue for a moment, and let the butter drip down your chin.

Raspberry
Harvesting

I began my raspberry harvesting career just off Main Street in Orem, Utah. I soon learned that what I had hoped would be an easy way for a teenager to make some spending money was really hot, tiring, back-breaking, tedious work. I found that big, purple-red raspberries came with a price — scratches on my arms, slivers in my fingers, mud on my shoes, and sweat everywhere else.

The first day of picking wasn't so bad. I ate more than I put in the crate. By the second day I had figured out that I needed to put more in the crate than in my mouth if I wanted to make any money. The third day, my crusty, wise supervisor taught me the secret.

As I struggled along the well-trimmed row of bushes, my supervisor watched me. Then she adjusted her sun hat and walked over to where I was picking. Without any fanfare, she squatted down next to me and spoke in a whisper.

"When you know how to pick raspberries," she said without looking up at me, "then you really know how to live.

"You can go along just like you are up there. But then you miss most of the best parts. But if you get down on your knees and look up, you'll see the biggest, juiciest berries that were hidden from un upright view."

I squatted near the supervisor and saw all kinds of berries hidden beneath the canopy of green leaves. Then my supervisor picked a few berries and put them into the bucket hanging on a rope around my waist. She was gray-haired and wrinkled, but she could pick as fast with one hand as I could with both.

"You know when a raspberry is ready," she continued. "It falls at a touch into your opened palm. But it takes the right touch. Not a pull or a tug, but a gentle touch, and when the raspberry's ready, it just lets go.

"God has that touch, and you know, my time's a-coming before long. When he comes picking, he'll know and I'll know when it's all right for me to let go. But I don't know if I'm quite ready. I'm like this pinkish one here. I've still got a lot of cling left in me yet."

At that moment, I still had sweat on my forehead, mud on my shoes, and scratches on my arms and hands, but suddenly raspberry harvesting changed for me.

Now if I want to find out something important about people, I try this experiment. I ask, "Who wants to pick raspberries?" Then I look around the room and see if anybody's eyes light up. If they do, I know they share my secret.

When you know how to pick raspberries, you really know how to live.

Babies, Budgets, and Bylines

"When do you find time to write?" a friend asked me after my newest baby and book came off the production line at almost precisely the same moment. I never know how to answer that question because I've never been able to *find* time to write. And let me tell you, I've looked everywhere.

Mingling personal time to do anything with raising a family is like putting oil and vinegar in a salad dressing jar . . . you have a hard time keeping them together. And it takes a lot of juggling and constant mix-ups to keep them well blended.

I published several articles and stories before I started my family. But after my first daughter was born, I thought I was too busy to write. So I put my writing on hold until I was "less busy."

About a year later, when my second daughter appeared before my first daughter had learned to walk, I found out my life didn't seem to be getting any less busy.

I figured out there was probably some kind of pattern developing here. I planned to have a large family. Even if I just waited until all the children were in school, that might be twenty or more years down the road. That seemed like a long time to put myself on hold.

I noticed it was never hard to find time to eat. I had even been prompted to call in the CIA to find my waistline after seven pregnancies in eight years. So why was finding time to write so hard?

It dawned on me that I *made* time to eat. I made time for the things highest on my list of priorities. Maybe I could make time to write.

That desire, coupled with my obstetrician's and pediatrician's desire to have me pay my bills, got me started in the baby, budget, and byline business. I must admit it's an unusual blending of careers. But it's one that offers me a unique challenge.

"I used to write, too," one mother of young children said to me. "But with all the interruptions, I can't seem to find any quiet time to get anything done."

I used to think interruptions were a problem, too. So one Saturday I had my husband take all the kids to town so I could have some peace and quiet and get some serious writing done. It was so quiet it completely disrupted my mind's unorganized coping methods. I couldn't seem to type without my two-year-old daughter standing guard right next to me. She loved to reach up and add a few extra letters to my manuscripts when I wasn't looking. (And my editors thought I made those typos.) I couldn't even get the right typing rhythm going without my infant son draped over my syncopated bouncing knees.

I began to accept the fact that constant interruptions were going to be a reality in my life for a long time to come. Oddly enough, I even got sort of used to them and could hardly work without them.

Over the years, my children have provided me with resource material for all the creative writing I want to do. They have kept up a steady pace of appearances, and their pacifiers and dirty sneakers have kept me supplied with a steady store of ideas.

The ideal set-up? There have been times, I must admit, when I've had serious doubts about the blending of these professions. Like the time when I received a box full of my book *Is There Life After Birth?* in the mail. I was so excited I called for all my kids to come in from playing outside and take a look.

"Oh, Mom, do we have to?" my three-year-old son asked.

Since they didn't seem quite as excited about it as I was, I added a little extra motivation. "I'll give you all a chocolate chip!"

They came rumbling back into the house and put their brakes on right in front of me.

"Look, kids," I said, smiling from here to there, "this is your Mommy's book! Isn't that neat? Isn't that wonderful? Aren't you excited?"

"I want my chocolate chip," my son interrupted, unimpressed.

Later I tried again at the bookstore. "Look, kids, here's your mother's book," I said, proudly holding up a brand-new copy of A Sense of Wonder.

"Oh, we already have that one," my son responded. "Let's buy this one." He waved a copy of my chief competitor's latest.

Then there was the time I was seated next to another writer at an autograph party at one of the mall bookstores.

"Did you have to sink a lot of money into your book too?" the other writer asked seriously.

"Yes," I answered, thinking about the high cost of type paper.

"You know, the editor I hired to rework my manuscript was really expensive. And then there was the typist to type my manuscript on top of that. Even the baby-sitter I hire to take care of my children costs a lot these days. And that professional photographer's rates were outrageous. And then, of course, that oak paneling my husband bought for my office in our mansion ran up a big bill. My, but writing a book can be expensive."

"Oh, yeah," I said, with an image of my office running through my mind. My desk was a damaged door balanced across two worn-out end tables. My typewriter was an old manual borrowed from my father-in-law. Both the desk and typewriter were carefully crammed into the storage room with just barely enough room to squeeze in my thrift store chair. I am my own editor, typist, baby-sitter, and photographer.

"Oh, yes, the price of type paper is terrible," I answered, trying to act as professional as possible.

"What?" she asked. "Oh . . . and that too."

Then there was the radio talk show host who invited me to be the guest on his program. The reason? Was it my great literary genius? Or perhaps it was my expert parenting techniques? No.

He had read several of my articles and parts of my books and had found out that all six of my children, along with their six beds and chest of drawers, were stacked on top of each other in one small bedroom of our small house. He had also learned that I don't jog at 5:00 A.M., and my three-year-old isn't a virtuoso on the violin. I'm not the PTA president or even the March of Dimes chairman for my block. He found out I am the very average, very exhausted mother of a house full of children who tells it like it is.

"I asked you to be on my program because you seem just like the rest of us," the talk show host said.

Combining bylines, budgets, and Baadsgaard raising is a delicate art. But I must admit, it's worth it—especially the Baadsgaard part.

One month, I had a book, articles, and stories published in every market I had been working for. The phone rang off the wall bringing praise from many sources. The mailbox was full, and there was even a little money in the checking account.

It was great to get to that point because it had taken years of hard work. But as the days passed, the phone calls slowed down, and the thrill of publishing began to fade. Writing had brought some immediate rewards of renown and remuneration. But I knew that even my best published projects were limited in ability, scope, and influence.

Then I looked at my children. Nothing I could ever hope to write or paint or compose could come close to the creation of a child.

So on those days when I wonder when or if I'll accomplish anything of importance . . . if I'll ever get caught up on the laundry . . . if I'll ever get that oft-rejected article or book published . . . then I remember I can count myself in the company of any of the masters of any of the arts. I am, day by day, accomplishing the highest of all art, the greatest of life's work. My children are my finest work, my personal masterpieces.

Nobody Has It All Together

I know I am the only mother on the planet who has oily hair, warts, and hairy legs. All the other mothers are sleek and beautiful. If they're not beautiful, they're probably smart, rich, or humble, or they do their genealogy.

That's why I always get a good belly laugh when I'm asked to speak about my books. Invariably, after my talk some soft-spoken woman in the group will approach me hesitantly and say something like, "You have everything so together. You are so calm and composed. I can tell you've been to one of those total-image beauty workshops where they drape you to find out your season, tell you what kind of clothes and makeup to wear, and how to style your hair."

I have to set the record straight. I am not so "together." As a matter of fact, if they quit manufacturing masking tape, I'd fall apart.

When I leave home to give a talk, I throw my husband a soup can, a screaming baby, a toddler with messy pants, and a smile, and say, "He-he-he . . . good-bye, dear."

The reason I seem calm and composed when I talk is because speaking to a hundred quiet, attentive adults is a piece of cake after I've been trying to communicate with six inattentive, exasperating children all day.

The truth is, I have never been draped to find out my "season." I consider myself a woman for all seasons. What's more, it's a lot more fun to imagine how much better I would look if I did go through the treatment, than to pay all that money and be disappointed because I still look this bad.

The rest of the truth is, I bought my suit on sale at Lerner's for $28.59. I did not select it because it was the perfect style for my figure or because it would do wonders for my image. I selected it because it was cheap and because dark gray hides spit-up stains. I don't wear designer pantyhose. I'm still wearing my old maternity pantyhose with a run in the thigh that no one can see. My ten-year-old shoes are held together with masking tape and hair spray.

My mother gave me a home perm and my husband tries to cut my hair. They have grand illusions of turning me into one of those before-and-after beauty studies like the women's magazines love to publish. So far, I am still the perfect specimen for the before photograph.

If not exactly stylish, at least I'm basically clean. Would that I could say the same thing of my children. I tell them often (when their father's not around) that they couldn't have acquired their dirty genes from my side of the family.

I have found, to my regret, that my children came self-equipped with more than dirty jeans. They came with dirty everything. With an uncanny green-thumb ability, they grow moldy socks in the dark crevices underneath their beds. They can take a half hour in the bathtub and still come out with tricycle grease smeared from their foreheads to their chins.

I have seen other people's children with every hair in place, spotless shoes, scrubbed faces, and matching socks. They must know a way to have children and cleanliness in the same place. I wanted to learn their secrets, so I decided to conduct an on-the-spot interview with one of these perfect parents. I sat down by a fountain at the shopping mall and waited.

One young woman walked past me holding her two-year-old daughter's hand. The little girl had blond ringlets dangling from lace barrettes and satin ribbons. Her solidly starched dress stood out from her clean, dimpled knees.

The little girl's stockings were not even bagging at the ankles.

"Miracle mother," I said, approaching this woman, "how do you do it?"

She looked around for cameras and replied, "I give her a box of bandages to rip open and plaster all over herself while I curl her hair. Then I give her an extra dose of cough medicine with antihistamine to keep her a little lethargic while I quickly dress her and speed over to the photographer's. But I only do this once every ten years."

The next mother came by with eight children following close behind her like a stepladder. They all resembled each other, so I assumed they were all hers. They were all clean, dressed, alert, and smiling. It was only 9:00 A.M. on a Saturday.

"How do you do it?" I asked as I stopped this amazing mother. "How do you get eight children up, clean, dressed, and over to the mall by 9:00 A.M.?"

"Well," she answered, "after I bathe them at night, I simply dress them for the next day and put them to bed that way. When they wake up, they're dressed and ready to go."

I scratched my head.

"It works the other way, too," the mother continued. "If you put them to bed in pajamas, then don't bother getting them dressed in the morning. If they stay in their pajamas all day, you don't have to get them ready to go to bed at night."

Next a mother and father walked by with four spotless young children all dressed in matching raincoats. Funny, I hadn't noticed any storm clouds on my way over. I questioned the father.

"Oh, we're going out to eat," the father said. "When we're through, I just take them all outside and hose them off."

So much for my visions of perfect parents up at dawn to bathe, bake, and bask in their perfection. I guess we're all in the same mud hole after all.

Hold On

Tired and weary from holding her fussy seven-month-old baby brother, my nine-year-old daughter, April, said in exasperation, "Jake, you're just going to have to learn how to suffer for a little while."

Suffering is foreign to Jacob right now. If he cries, someone picks him up. If he's hungry, someone feeds him. If he's tired, someone puts him to bed.

Still covered with a few scabs from a recent bout with chicken pox, April has a limited but expanded view of suffering just now. A few weeks ago, after hours of baking-soda baths, hugs, medication, and calamine lotion, April cried to me for more relief.

"I'm sorry, April," I told her as I held her on my lap. "There's nothing more I can do for you. Just try to stand it. You should feel better by tomorrow."

But tomorrow came and April didn't feel better. She felt worse. Her entire body, inside and out, was covered with chicken pox blisters. Her temperature soared. After all the usual tries to comfort her had failed, I realized that she needed guidance in how to endure.

I took April to the window and pointed to the plum tree in our backyard. There had been a big windstorm the night before and piles of tiny green plums covered the ground underneath the tree.

Then I called April's attention to the top of the plum tree. There, in the leaf-covered branches, a few tiny green plums were still clinging tightly to the tree. They had survived the storm and would be able to draw strength from the tree throughout the growing season. They would grow and ripen and live to see the harvest.

"Sometimes, for the present," I said, turning to April, "all we can do is hold on. Sometimes it's that ability, and that ability alone, that gets us through the rough parts. But if we do hold on, then eventually the storm does pass and the sun comes out and we can go on again."

April looked at me and then she looked back to the tree. She didn't say anything, but I knew she understood.

"You can draw on the strength of someone beyond yourself, beyond your parents, and beyond this world," I continued. "No one has to suffer alone."

That evening, when the pain reached its peak, I noticed April kneeling at the side of her bed.

The blistered inflamed, pus-filled pox sores started to scab over and heal in the next few days. April began comforting her younger brothers and sisters, who had come down with the same disease.

Like April, I have had to learn to hold on. But watching her suffer was new to me, something no one had prepared me for. Maybe the greatest pain in life is not our own, but standing back with anxious, idle hands when there is nothing more we can do, and watching our children hurt.

Last evening, I walked up to the plum tree in our backyard. The tiny plums the windstorm had blown off the tree a few weeks ago were yellow, hard, and wrinkled, almost disappearing in the grass. The plums still clinging to the tree had grown. Their firm, shiny green skins were starting to glow from the inside with the same soft light of the setting sun.

Vacation Time?

I find that life is much easier when you're not supposed to be having fun.

The dictionary says a vacation is a "time of respite from something, a scheduled period during which activity is suspended; a period of exemption from work granted for rest and relaxation."

It is obvious that this noted author of word definitions never took a vacation with children. If you've tried taking a vacation with kids, you know what I mean. The only activity a vacation with kids suspends is rest and relaxation.

My husband and I have been naive enough to take all kinds of vacations over the years. You'd think we'd learn.

Our first vacation together, more commonly known as the honeymoon, was definitely not restful or relaxing. This is probably what caused our next type of vacation: the family vacation.

Just thinking about our last family vacation gives me the hives. By the time we had packed enough bottles, diapers, and food to keep our kids happy for a few hours, there wasn't any room left in our car for passengers. We hadn't even pulled all the way out of the driveway before we heard, "Mom, aren't we there yet?"

"I've got to go."

"Tell Jordan to quit touching me."

But my husband and I had made a vow: "We will have a good time with the kids if it kills us!" Little did we know that it nearly would.

We started out with an idealistic dream of romantic palm trees swaying in the breeze as we lounged on the beach. What we got was a kid who came down with motion sickness during "Star Tours" in Disneyland.

We started our vacation with an image of happy children singing songs as we sped down the freeway to vacationland. What we got was a major wrestling match in the back seat.

I started out saying sweet things like, "Oh, children, won't this be exciting?" I later found myself screaming, "I don't care if his skin is touching you. If you kids don't quit fighting, I'm going to push both your heads out the window and let your lips flap you to death!"

I started out the trip lovingly wrapping my arms around my sweet, darling children. By the end of the trip, I was wearing earplugs, taking medication, and carefully mapping out boundary lines with black tape down the middle of the car seat.

Why do we do it? Why do we fight the crowds at Disneyland, on the freeway, or at the beach? Because we are having fun as a family. If it kills us, we are going to have a close family, starting now.

But real fun on family vacations has a way of coming at the oddest moments. It comes while your skin is stuck to the seat with your child's purple gum and you suddenly don't care anymore. You start throwing Twinkies into the back seat and sticking your toes out the window.

After my daughter kicked her brother and he punched her back in front of 35,000 people waiting in line for Dumbo the Flying Elephant, I said, "What's the matter with you kids? Don't you have any pride, fighting in front of all these people like this?"

"Well, Mom," my daughter answered, "they don't know it's us."

Maybe that's where the fun comes in. If nobody knows it's us, we can behave like ourselves both in private and in public.

I've asked my friends with teenagers in their families what vacations are like. They told me things don't get any better. They said they still pretend not to notice the comments from the back seat: "How come we had to come on this dumb trip, anyway?"

"I can't believe we had to drive a thousand miles to see that."

"Tell John to keep his shoes on. He's stinking up the whole car."

Another friend of mine told me she had traveled barely ten miles from her home on a family vacation when a police car pulled them over. After a heated discussion, she found out her son had put a sign in the back window that read, "Help me! I'm being kidnapped!"

When I was growing up, my father and mother always insisted we have the annual summer family vacation. We had such a big family we had to take two cars, and sometimes we had a hard time staying together. After my sister was left in a gas station rest room in Las Vegas and we didn't even notice until we hit Provo, our family vacations seemed to get fewer and farther between.

My two-year-old son kept yelling, "I want to go home! I want to go home!" every five seconds on our most recent family vacation. He puts it well. Vacations give us, after all, something to go home from. Home never looked so good.

Why Does My Mother's Day Potted Plant Always Die?

For a few weeks before Mother's Day, kids all over the country start wondering what to get Mom for her special day.

It's only right that children should wonder about their mothers for a few weeks a year. After all, mothers are wondering all year long about the kids. Moms all over the planet continually ask themselves, "Why is it that a child who forgets to do his homework, who can't even remember to flush the toilet, can remember exactly how much allowance *he* got when *he* was in the first grade?"

When a woman has her first baby, she becomes a mother. Easy enough. When she lets emotion overrule reason and has baby number 2, she suddenly becomes a referee, only she doesn't get to wear a striped shirt, blow a whistle, or control the game.

The moment baby number 2 is born, baby number 1 approaches Mother in the recovery room of the hospital with "The Sibling Bill of Rights." Mother will never fully recover because of it.

From this time on and forevermore, Mother must count the M & M's to make sure each child gets exactly the same amount. For the rest of her mothering career, she is subjected to acute sibling attacks.

This strange malady works like this: If one child gets a present or treat or any personal attention, the other child immediately starts clenching his jaw muscles. His eyeballs flash red lasers and smoke shoots out his ears while a voice says, "Why is *his* ice-cream cone bigger than mine?"

This child cannot remember to bring his gym clothes home to get washed, but he can tell you exactly what Grandma gave him for his birthday when he was thirteen. Ask a child his multiplication facts and his mind may slip on one or two. But ask him whose turn it is to sit by the window in the car and you have bull's-eye accuracy.

The same child who is having trouble with measurement principles in math at school can tell you up to a micromillimeter who has the biggest piece of cake after supper. He can weigh bowls of cereal to see who got the most by balancing the bowls in both his hands while sticking out his tongue to test and allow for the wind factor.

There is really no way for Mother to win in this war. She began the losing battle when she allowed into her mind the naive thought, "Junior really needs a little brother to play with." From that point on, the only advantage she has in the fight is that she never has to employ spies.

"Mom! Jeff's been stuffing his dirty socks down the heat vents again!"

"Mom! Ann's hiding her snail collection in the toilet tank!"

Mothers never win. Just when you're finally starting to get used to waking up at 2:00 A.M. to feed the baby, the kid starts sleeping through the night. Just when you finally get diapering down to a science, the kid gets toilet trained. Just when you get really good at giving terrific birthday parties, the kid asks you to hide in your bedroom during his party so that you won't embarrass him in front of his friends. Just when your kid stops getting embarrassed when you come out of your bedroom, he moves away to go to college. By the time you finally know how to put on one heck of a wedding, all the kids are married off.

And don't be fooled. You can't pass along all that good stuff you learned when the kids have their own kids, because the in-laws think you're butting in where you're not invited if you give unsolicited advice. So you sit back and watch your kids make the same mistakes with their kids that you did with them, and you bite your tongue a lot.

Just when you think you're not going to worry about all this mother stuff anymore, one of the kids comes back home to stay and brings along the wife and seven kids.

On Mother's Day in church, people make you stand up and admit it. Then they give you a potted plant in perfect health, which you somehow always manage to kill in three days flat. You begin to wonder if that plant is somehow symbolic of your mothering abilities.

Always, without fail, someone will stand up in church on Mother's Day and say something like, "My mother never, oh, no, never, oh, not even one little time . . . raised her voice in our home."

You start to slink down in your seat and mumble something you hope no one can hear, but at the same time you want to jump up on your seat and scream, "What would she do if your pants were on fire?"

Before I became a mother, I always looked critically at other people's children and thought, "My children will never, no never, have unattended runny noses, limp bangs hanging in their eyes, or thumbs stuck disgustingly in their mouths." The other day I looked at my children. One had an unattended runny nose, one had limp bangs hanging in her eyes, and two others were disgustingly sucking their thumbs. Sometimes I wonder if maybe I should have been a nun.

When Rudyard Kipling wrote, "If you can keep your head when all about you are losing theirs and blaming it on you; if you can trust yourself when all men doubt you but make allowances for their doubting too . . . " I think he had mothers in mind.

So while all the kids are wondering for a few short weeks what to get Mom for her special day, Mom is still, as always, wondering about the kids. No, she isn't wondering why she had you and your brother or sister. She's wondering why at one minute she feels such tenderness swell inside her, she can barely contain it without cradling you — then at another minute she hears herself yelling, "Why don't you grow up?"

She's wondering why after all the things she said that you didn't listen to, you chose to listen to that one — "Grow up!" — and you did.

She knows the love she feels for you and your brother or sister is complete. She knows her love can't be divided up like a pie, with everybody getting a piece exactly the same size.

Every child gets the whole pie.

The Spirit Was Willing

If you want to feel old, go back to school when you're a middle-aged mother of six. If you want to feel ancient, enroll in P.E. 129 (Fitness for Life) at BYU when you're a middle-aged mother of six.

Talk about intimidating! This class curriculum makes a college-level course out of telling people how fat and worn out they are. Now, I already know how fat and worn out I am. It's just that I've never had special numbers to emphasize the bare facts.

When my instructor, Fitness Fred, stood up in front of my first physical education class in twelve years and said he was going to pinch me and make me run eleven laps on the inside track of the Smith Fieldhouse, I decided to plead medical hardship. I approached him at the end of the class period with my speech mentally prepared.

"I've just crawled off the delivery table, after seven difficult pregnancies," I pleaded. "Surely you can't mean for me to run eleven laps."

"Does your family have a history of sudden heart attacks?" instructor Fred asked in reply.

Now, I wasn't worried about my family history at that moment. I was worried about mine. But I answered truthfully. "No," I replied.

"Run the laps," Mr. Fitness said with a stone serious face. "You will feel pain, and I don't mean the childbirth kind."

I dutifully followed my dedicated instructor's instructions and set out for the Smith Fieldhouse indoor track. The first thing I noticed was an overabundance of toned young athletes doing very little sweating or huffing and puffing. What is a woman to do who hasn't even worn a pair of shorts for twelve years? I rolled up my pants, exposing my white legs flecked with razor stubble, complete with white anklets and orthopedic shoes.

I approached the rack with my best "Rocky" expression, breathing deeply. I took a look at the clock next to the women's rest room, and began.

I got about halfway around the first lap before I ran totally out of gas. "Just ten and a half left to go," I told myself. "Piece of cake. Go for it, Big Jan." That was the last time I was coherent for the duration of the ordeal. Severe lack of oxygen can do strange things to a person's mind. My half-conscious brain waves kept pleading with my legs, "Please, you guys. Just one more step."

Don't get me wrong. I've always believed in physical fitness. It's just that every time I went out for a run in the past, my obstetrician put me to bed with premature labor.

I gave it everything I had. Without stopping, I ran the entire Herculean marathon. Twenty minutes later, I dragged my barely breathing body over the finish line. I couldn't believe it. I did it. I didn't die.

After a very lengthy cool down, I grabbed my class manual and eagerly searched for the table that would tell me how I did. I was rather proud of myself until I read my fitness rating.

"If you run 1.5 miles in 19:31," the manual read, "your fitness category is . . . VERY POOR."

I naively thought the run would be the worst part of the course until I showed up for class the next day. That was where the pinching part came in. I had to borrow a pair of shorts from my ten-year-old daughter for the ordeal.

The first thing I thought about before the fat pinching test was the chocolate ice cream banana split I had eaten the night before. The next thing I noticed was the pincher. My instructor took out a device that looked as if it had been invented during the days when prison torture was legal in this country. Fred tried to reassure me it was a simple, painless test. He would simply pinch my fat and measure it. All these numbers added together would tell him what percent of my body was made up of fat.

I thought *that* was private information a woman only tells herself when she looks in the mirror when no one is around.

I explained this to my instructor, but he didn't seem to hear me as he grabbed hunks of my side, thigh, and arm. Then he wrote a bunch of numbers down on a piece of paper and told me I was dismissed.

The next part of this exciting class period consisted of being weighed and measured. It's not enough to know you're not even up to very poor in your cardiovascular endurance test, and that a large part of your body consists of fat. Now you have to know how tall you are and how much you weigh.

After you have all this useful information about yourself, you're supposed to do something about it. A contract is now in order. In my case, I was able to choose whether I wanted to work on my fat or my severe lack of endurance.

Now, this is a very detailed contract. You contract for how fast you are going to make your heart beat while you huff and puff your way to better health. You even have to decide how long you want to do this each day, and you have to mark down the days, weeks, and type of exercise you want to commit to. Most of the rest of the course, they told me, is on my honor.

Students who have honor are supposed to show progress by the end of a six-week exercise program. At this point, Fred grabs your fat and makes you run eleven laps again. If you don't show any progress, you get a big fat F.

The walk down that long hall of the Richards Building after class seemed monumental. Near the front of the building is a plaque in bronze that reads, "The human body is sacred — the veritable tabernacle of the divine spirit which inhabits it. It is a solemn duty of mankind to develop, protect, and preserve it from pollution, unnecessary wast-age and weakness." (Stephen L Richards.) There is a very large, solemn portrait of Stephen L Richards next to this plaque. I felt like a blimpy marshmallow when I looked up into his eyes. But I was determined.

I promised myself that when I reentered that building at the end of my six-week program for fat, weak people, I would enter in style. With a towel slung over my tanned, toned shoulders, I planned to climb those entrance steps with an orchestra playing "Ms. Rocky" in the background.

On second thought, I decided to leave out the raw eggs in my morning milkshake.

Nothing Tenderizes Like Fatherhood

They were all looking for just the right Father's Day card, but none of the cards on the department-store shelf seemed to say what they felt. The father of their children deserved more than store-bought sentimentality.

First there was Ned. His wife was looking for a "new father" card. She had just given birth to their first child last week—a son. Ned was tending his boy for the first time. He still had bloodshot eyes.

Twenty-two-year-old Ned had no idea what it took to get a baby born. When they handed him his new son, still wet and wide-eyed in the delivery room, something happened inside.

"I'm a father . . . I have a son," he thought to himself, almost afraid to let the delivery room nurse discern his thoughts as he awkwardly cradled his new son. He ventured a finger on the soft pink cheek. But the skin was so soft he could barely feel it with his calloused, working man's hands.

"I'm a father . . . " The words kept ringing through his mind.

A whole new set of values swept over him. Their tiny apartment and his motorcycle suddenly changed into hopes for a station wagon and a home of their own, with a swing in the backyard.

Then there was Robert. His wife had just left to go shopping for his Father's Day gift on a Saturday afternoon. He was tending the kids. He was getting pretty good at it by now. He could tell a story to the one-year-old, insist that the four-year-old quit pinching his sister, keep his eye on the six-year-old just learning to ride his bike, and tell the eight-year-old which note she missed on the piano — all while diapering the baby.

He had unknowingly developed expertise in fixing tricycles, bandaging scraped knees, and bathing all five small children at once in five minutes. He could make pancakes into child-pleasing animal shapes and spin a bedtime story to enthrall an audience varying in interest levels from bottles and pacifiers to lip gloss and boyfriends.

Then there was Stan. His wife was looking for just the right card to express her feelings.

Just when Stan finally thought he had diapering perfected, the kid started asking for the car keys. Nobody wanted to be thrown in the air anymore when Stan got home from work. He was suddenly no longer a marvelous magician because he could make the car lights turn on by touching his nose.

Now he had to fight to get a few minutes in the bathroom before leaving for work. Somebody was always "borrowing" his razor and asking him to please update his wardrobe.

But there were other times when he knew he still had an important job. Like the time when Amy didn't get a date for the junior prom and he took her on a special date instead. Or when Stan Jr. didn't make the basketball team. There were the struggles to come up with money for tuition and the graduations.

Then there was Albert. His wife was looking for just the right grandpa card.

Just when Albert thought nobody needed his expertise in diapering, tending to scraped knees, and mending broken hearts, he suddenly found himself with a brand-new title. People are calling him "grand" these days. And it's a title he well deserves.

The same son who had called him "the old man" and thought Albert knew less than nothing about anything is now suddenly asking him, with a new humbled reverence, how to take care of diaper rash.

"How did you do it, Dad?" is a phrase he hears a lot these days. And he can sit back and talk about the lean years, the high rent, keeping food on the table and shoes on the kids, to a quiet audience that displays new interest.

Then there is Nathan. He's home tending again today as his wife, daughter, and granddaughter shop for gifts for their "dads." His newest great-grandson is cradled in his arms, a tiny four-week-old infant drifting slowly to sleep.

Those same old feelings come swelling to the surface. The same awe he felt years ago in the delivery room of the hospital now envelops him. He ventures to stretch a wrinkled finger over to touch the soft cheek. Nathan has recently been given a still newer title. People are calling him "great" as well as "grand" these days.

When the baby wakes and restlessly cries with hunger, Nathan quickly walks to the kitchen. After fixing the bottle, he tries out the formula temperature on his wrist. Laying the infant's head in the fold of his arm, the comfortable place, he begins to settle deep into the rocker and wonder a little about life and death. All the pieces start to come together, and the puzzle starts to show the whole picture now.

AUTUMN

Autumn comes twice.

First, in the mountains, the season of fire appears. One day you look up and realize the green has gone out; summer's over.

Then, as if to give you a second chance, autumn comes again. The reds, yellows, and oranges that were once only in the mountains flow like honey to the valley floor. Slowly, each tree in the valley begins to glow from the inside out, finally exploding in a mass of color.

One day you look up and school has snatched your children. You think the season ended, childhood over. Then one afternoon your little boy comes home from school, a young man, sits in the chair, and talks to you like a human being.

The season is not past. It's just beginning.

Teacher, Don't Blow Out This Light

Every year when the first day of school rolls around, I find myself mentally preparing a letter to send to my child's new teacher. If I ever have the courage to send such a letter, it will probably read something like this:

Dear Teacher,

Today I am not so willingly handing over to you my most treasured possession. She may not look like much to you, with her flyaway hair, toothless grin, and socks that always fall down around her ankles. But let me tell you, she happens to be, without a doubt, the most wonderful child who has ever graced this planet.

She forgets to brush her teeth and flush, but she never forgets to find wonder in the smallest ray of sunlight on water. She'll remember to brush her teeth and flush soon enough. But please don't let her forget the wonder.

She never notices the mess in her bedroom. But boy, how she notices the way leaves bend in the wind and the delicate softness of a new blade of grass. She'll learn to see the messes soon enough. But please don't let her forget about the grass and the wind.

She has trouble with her J's. She always writes them backward. But you should see her with a blank sheet of paper and a crayon or paintbrush in her hand. There is more life, color, and exuberance in her paintings and drawings than in all those millions of mass-produced color re-productions over everyone's sofas. She'll learn to write her J's correctly soon enough. But please don't let her forget her excitement for the feel of wet paint and the smell of wax crayons.

I know she tends to ask a lot of questions: "Why can't we see the wind?" or "What are stars?" Please don't let her forget to ask questions.

My daughter will not be bringing a set of expert reading or math skills to your classroom today. But she is bringing something far more important. She is bringing you a curious mind.

Someday in the future, I would like to see her emerge from your mountains of drills, papers, and tests with something more important than accumulated knowledge. I hope she will emerge with the desire to know and an ability to really see what she possesses now.

She may not know her multiplication tables or how to diagram a sentence. But you see, she already knows how to be puzzled, to wonder and question, how to be observant, spontaneous, playful, and free. She is open to new experiences and can look freshly at common things.

I know she may not look very smart to you. But the things that are most important, she already knows.

Please allow her to keep what she brings to you today.

Sincerely,
Your new student's mother

'Tis the Season for Bottles Chanting, "Fill Me, Fill Me"

Just when you get your kids out from under your feet and back in school, you notice your Kerr jars have been reproducing while you had your back turned all summer. Your storage-room shelves are filled with empty glass bottles that now wake you up at midnight chanting, "Fill me . . . fill me . . . fill me . . . or you will never be able to hold up your head in Relief Society again."

Of course, you have forgotten the vow you made last year as you stood in the middle of your kitchen floor, stuck to the linoleum with gobs of fruit syrup. "I vow never to do this again," you swore with your rusty fruit peeler over your heart, your pears turning brown in the sink, your baby screaming from his crib, and the electric power suddenly shut off because of a thunderstorm. "It's not worth it. I'll take my sanity, drive down to the supermarket, and buy my fruit in neat little cans."

Then you remember you don't even like bottled or canned fruit. You just eat it all the time because nobody else in the family will and you'll be darned if you're going to let all your hard work go to waste.

. Why are you going to break your vow again this year? I'll tell you why.

Deciding to can fruit is like finding out you're pregnant. At first you get all excited and dream about holding that soft, sweet little newborn in your arms.

Nine months later, you find yourself on the delivery table. "Why?" you wonder. "Why did I forget what it takes to get a baby here?"

With canning fruit, you remember all those bright, shiny, red, orange, and yellow fruit-filled bottles lined up neatly on your storage-room shelf, ready for your winter cooking. Or some "friend" drops off bushels of "free" fruit, and you don't want to let it spoil. So you dig in again.

Hours later, when you're knee-deep in peach pits, your toddler is skiing across the kitchen floor on pear slices, and your husband impatiently asks, "What's for dinner?" you throw your rusty fruit peeler over your heart and vow again.

Something has helped me through the canning season guilt trip. I figure there are two ways for food to "go to waste." The first way is if you let it spoil. The second way is to eat it and let it go to your "waist."

So I still drive up to the local fruit orchard and buy the bushels of ripe fruit so I'll fit in at Relief Society. But when I get home, I encourage the kids to have their fill. If they eat all the fruit before I can get to it, I act frustrated so they'll feel guilty. Then I don't have to.

I used to tell the children, "Don't eat that fruit. I have to wash it, peel it, stuff it in jars, dump sugar on it, and cook it for you first."

The second way is a lot easier.

Real Mothers Endure

Everybody has a mother. That cross, forty-six-year-old, pot-bellied neighbor of yours was once carried for nine months beneath someone's heart. That obnoxious co-worker once had fat pink toes that someone cradled and kissed. As difficult as it is to realize, every stranger we see on the street, and each person in all the masses that cover the earth, is separately and uniquely someone's child.

Every mother soon learns for herself that each child comes with the message that God is not entirely discouraged with us—that life should go on. Each time a new baby is born, a mother is created. But real mothering goes far beyond the process of birth. Birth is only the beginning point for two unique, separate individuals, the mother and child, to grow, change, and mature together.

Real mothers, contrary to many Sunday School Mother's Day tributes, are not always heroic and strong. Real mothers are not perfect examples of every human virtue.

Real mothers burn the toast and undercook the roast. Real mothers sometimes lose their patience and their minds. Real mothers sometimes feel overwhelmed and discouraged.

But real mothers endure. Real mothers hang in there. Their love is not conditional. Real mothers seldom send in their resignations, stating, "This is too hard. I don't want to be a mother anymore. I quit."

Real mothers seldom exchange even their most difficult

children because they are not pleased with the merchandise.

Real mothers spend their lives providing roots, then allowing their children to branch out and flower into their own lives. For real mothers know that this is the only way fruit will come to provide the good seed for the next generation.

People who have read my books for parents of young children sometimes ask me when I'm going to write one about teenagers. I laugh and they laugh. Then we pat each other on the back and part company. But there have been times when our conversations have gone deeper. What I often find in these conversations is a very discouraged, disheartened parent behind the facade.

Almost without exception these parents have a child who has chosen to abandon their rules and values. My children aren't teenagers yet, so I don't know if they will choose to follow my way of life. That is the most disquieting thing about this parenthood business. There is no certainty. Some of us will struggle through colic, potty training, birthday parties, Little League, and dating, only to find our child has grown up to be a drunken wife abuser.

Although in the majority of cases good parenting produces relatively stable, trouble-free adults, there are no guarantees. Even in the best cases, most of the rewards of parenting are long in coming. In the worst cases, the rewards don't seem to come at all.

We parents are all amateurs. But I do believe that all our effort, loving, and caring do count, if not for the child, then unknowingly for ourselves.

Parents aren't allowed to choose their children. They don't get to go to the market and purchase the nicest package, with a "return if not fully satisfied" guarantee label. But most parents still make the conscious choice to accept whatever they get, no questions asked. Most choose to love, to care, to never give up.

Parents are not logical or practical with their emotions, their time, or their resources. They give all they have to every child. So, in spite of what the child becomes, the parents have unknowingly transformed themselves.

The parents I have talked to have had real, tangible, deep pain in their eyes and quiet humility in their voices. These parents have changed from people knowing all the answers to people asking the questions. They have become what we all should be: searching, questioning, nonjudgmental human beings.

Their child may not have chosen to follow their way of life, and so they feel like failures. They do not see what I see in them. I see parents who have not given up their values. Those values have led them to never give up, to never quit hoping, to ever keep loving their child. In that loving, a love that expects no acceptance, no return or repayment, they have attained the greatest quality of character in mankind.

In these parents, I see true greatness. And if I ever write a book about teenagers, it will be your stories and your courage that will give it life.

Driving Force

She watched her teenage son racing to the family station wagon after church, yanking his tie and suit coat off in one smooth motion. "Come on, Mom," he called back as he rolled down the window. "Get yourself in gear. Let's make tracks." He gunned the ignition.

She turned to me. "He's driving," she said. "I can't believe he's driving. I try not to act nervous when he's behind the wheel. I only told him sixteen times to start slowing down *before* he gets to the stop signs."

He gunned the motor again and waved her on.

"He says I don't have enough confidence in him," she continued. "I have confidence in him—I think. But he just doesn't understand that it seems like yesterday when I was trying to get him to use the potty chair that made music when he produced." She gripped her scriptures until her knuckles went white. "I will not gasp," she repeated to herself. "I will not jam my right foot down on the passenger side looking for an extra brake pedal. I will let his father drive with him. I will walk home from church."

She relaxed. "Go ahead, son," she called to him. "I'll meet you at home later." Then her voice trailed off into a whisper. "Please be careful."

"What?" I asked.

"Oh, nothing," she said, covering her eyes with her Bible as her son screeched out of the parking lot.

"I thought I would have more time," she said, turning to me. "When did he grow up? I've been there every day. I just didn't notice. I'm not ready for this." She took a deep breath.

"You know, though, just the other day he came home after school, sat down on the kitchen table, and we talked for two hours like best friends. He's really something. I like him," she said, almost surprised with her own words. "I like my son. He's quite a young man. Now, if I can just get his father to drive with him . . . "

"How about a ride home?" I asked.

"Great," she answered. "I hate walking home in these high heels. They make my toes bleed. You know, my son said I ought to wear something more comfortable and practical, not just dress like everybody else my age. He said I shouldn't be afraid to be different. I think he has a point there."

Open. Close. Suction.

I try to put it off. I let spring and summer roll by trying to ignore it. Then November hits, and I realize I have to go through with it again. It's time for the annual family checkup at the dentist's office.

You see, it's not my kids I'm worried about. Kids these days get laughing gas, videos, rings, a new green Grover toothbrush, coupons for free french fries, and balloons. It's my part on the program that worries me. While my kids are out in the hallway deciding which ring or scratch-and-sniff sticker to choose, I'm left alone in the dentist's chair.

Because the dentist's time is so valuable, the dentist's assistant does most of the dirty work. After the assistant puts the paper bib around my neck, she always asks me to bite down on stiff paper squares that look like the rejects from someone's summer vacation slides. Next she throws an X-ray shield over my body that's heavy enough to suspend breathing. "Don't breathe," she smiles, as she steps out of the room to do something to me that she doesn't want to be around for. Then she steps back into the room and pulls the spit-covered slides out of my mouth and takes them to another room to develop . . . heaven knows what.

Later, the dentist and his assistant consult in the hall with low voices while they hold my negatives up to the light. This is the precursor to the rubber dam, a hot, slimy, smelly piece of plastic clamped to my face to "isolate the work place." I think it was really invented to keep patients from crying out or making snide remarks while they're under the drill.

As soon as this dam is in place, everyone disappears. My husband takes the kids home, the dentist and his assistant go out for lunch, and the receptionist runs out to pick up some more plastic fingernails.

I'm alone. I can't breathe, speak, or swallow.

Just when I know I've had my last breath, there he is, my smiling dentist. He makes some cheerful greeting while he opens drawers and assembles all his tools—one of which looks like the one I saw in the hands of the concrete repairman outside.

I have noticed that dentists generally fall into three conversational categories. The first type carries on a continual conversation with the assistant. You spend the whole visit wondering if he's paying attention to what he's doing. The second type says absolutely nothing except, "Open." "Close." And occasionally, "Suction."

The third type tries to carry on a conversation with the patient: "Well, Janene, how are things at the Baadsgaard house these days?" or "What do you think about the trouble in the Middle East?" There I am, my mouth crammed with hairy fingers, a large plastic suction tube, and a busy jackhammer. Saliva is accumulating under the rubber dam and trickling down my chin. Does he *really* want to know what I think—about anything? I spend the rest of the visit wondering if he wants me to blink once for terrific or twice for rotten.

Dentists remind me of my children. They work for a while, then they wander off. After they apply pink grit to every tooth during a cleaning, they advise you not to swallow. They say, "Well, let's let that set for a moment." Then they're off for an hour. Of course, you can hear them in the next room, laughing, talking, swallowing, making three hundred bucks.

My husband told me to call and make an appointment for the family this morning. I think I'll wait until tomorrow.

Back to School

It's time for the annual event parents dread at the end of every summer. It's called "Back to School" by the retailers. It's called torture by mothers.

First, take several free-spirited children who haven't been out of their cut-offs, T-shirts, and bare feet all summer. Second, take one organized, well-intentioned mother. Last, throw in a simple shopping trip to outfit free spirits for school. Add all these ingredients and you get one disaster.

The mother's first dilemma is whether or not to take the children along for the shopping trip. If you don't take the children, things will go much more smoothly, at least until you get home. Then you'll find out you bought all the wrong sizes or styles.

If you take the kids, you won't be able to walk into a store without lecturing: "Now, I don't want anybody touching anything. Look, don't touch. This is not our stuff. So keep your hands to yourselves. If anybody breaks anything, it comes out of your allowance for the next seventeen years. Mother does not carry no-fault insurance on any of you. I don't want anybody trying to go up the down escalator or goofing off in the elevators. If you have to go, tough. I already gave you a chance before we left home. I don't want any punching, poking, hitting, pulling, ripping, teasing, or loud burping."

Once a mother actually enters the store, any kid worth his salt knows how to play the game. Mom will yell at kids in the car or at home, but once inside the store, mothers restrain themselves. Now it's the kids' turn.

"Mom, can I have this? Huh? Can I? Can I?"

"I'm thirsty. I need a drink of water."

"I've got to go, Mom. Oh . . . OH . . . OH . . . REAL BAD!"

"I don't want to take off my clothes. What if someone *sees* me?"

"You never told me not to wear socks without holes in them. No, I can't remember the last time my socks got washed. What do you think I am, a genius? I don't think they smell that bad."

"Nobody wears gross things like that anymore, Mom. No way. I wouldn't be caught dead in that thing."

"I don't want to go into the dressing room *alone*."

"Mom, you don't have to go into the dressing room with me. Do you think I'm a baby or what?"

By the end of this back-to-school shopping trip, mothers and kids claim they don't know each other.

Once I was checking out the back-to-school specials at Pic 'N' Save when suddenly a terrifying alarm went off. Every shopper and employee froze and stood perfectly still. The cash registers stopped. The schmaltzy music stopped. Everything stopped, except my son Joseph. He ran toward me with panic in his eyes. Then he dodged behind a large box and peeked around the corner with a guilty look on his face.

An employee ran toward him. "Did you touch that?" she excitedly asked my son.

He put his eyebrows down and refused to answer her. The store clerk quickly pulled out a key and turned off the alarm. When I turned around, I noticed an entire store full of people staring, perfectly quietly, at Joseph and me.

I tried to slip away and deny my motherhood. But Joseph just kept following me.

Mothers of kindergarten children must face registration even before the first big school day. Once they get their child's birth certificate and a record of immunizations, most mothers think they're in the clear. This is definitely naive.

Now you have to go to your local elementary school

and fill out a pile of forms. You'll do pretty well on the part that asks you to fill in the parents' names, address, phone number, and zip code. But then you get to the hard part: "What is your occupation?"

I filled in "plumber" when I registered my oldest daughter for kindergarten. After all, I had retrieved thirteen toy trucks with a plunger earlier that morning.

I filled in "private investigator" when I registered my second daughter. I had been working on the mystery of the missing sneaker for months and had finally broken the case that day.

I filled in "major general" this last time. You wouldn't believe the wars we get in around my house.

Just when you think you've got this registration business all figured out, you'll see a question like this: "Describe the condition of your home. Check one: Excellent, good, moderate, fair, poor, broken."

How on earth do they expect you to answer a question like that? Even though I am considered happily married, I always check "broken." After all, everything *is* at my house: the washing machine, the screen door, the suitcase zipper on my temple clothes bag, the bikes, the drainpipes.

Now comes the first day of school. You spend a heart-stopping morning stuffing sun-tanned free spirits into stiff corduroys and squeaky shoes. All of a sudden you want to claim your motherhood rights for a little longer before you ship them off. This feeling, however, lasts only for a few moments.

Mothers of kindergarten children are a dead giveaway on the first day of school. I observed one middle-aged mother grinning from ear to ear on the first day of kindergarten. "This is the swan song, or the part where the fat lady sings, folks," she said gleefully, handing in her youngest child's immunization chart, birth certificate, and $12 snack fee. "This better not happen again," she said, "or the doctor will have to come up with the snack fee."

Another mother was signing up the last of her eight children with the same happy anticipation. She passed right by the table where enthusiastic first-time mothers were eagerly volunteering to be room mothers and parent helpers.

"I don't even feel a twinge of guilt," she said laughing. "I used to do everything with my first kids, but now I know better."

Mothers signing up their first children for kindergarten wear contrasting solemn expressions. When the new kindergarten teacher called these new parents to order in her orientation meeting, they listened attentively to her list of ABC's for kindergarten. On that list, "A for Animals" was followed by: "I don't mind if they come for show and tell, but they can't stay all day. Mom will have to bring them and take them home when show and tell is over." Seasoned parents know what the teacher really means: she doesn't enjoy finding runaway snakes in her desk drawer.

First-time parents look the new teacher over with a critical eye and ask a lot of questions. I overheard one new mother of a kindergartener instructing the teacher to call her son T. J. instead of Timothy. "He won't know you are talking to him if you use his real name," she said.

Seasoned parents ask what is the earliest time they can drop a child off. First-timers become nervous when the kindergarten teacher says the parents can't stay for the first day of class.

First-time parents naively adhere strictly to the school rules that say, "Students must not arrive at school before 8:45 A.M. and must leave no later than 3:00 P.M. because teachers have enough to do in the mornings and afternoons without having to baby-sit your child."

Seasoned parents are more likely to send a note to the school stating their home rules: "Students must leave home no later than 8:30 A.M. and not return home any earlier than 3:30. After all, we parents have enough to do in the mornings and afternoons without having to baby-sit your students."

New parents follow the teacher's rule that says everything the child wears or brings to school must be labeled so the child does not come home with two left shoes. Seasoned parents don't label anything, on the chance the child may come home with something better than he left with.

New parents listen to the teacher say: "Please take a quick look at your child as you kiss him good-bye. Check him for fever, rash, or chicken pox, or I may have to send him home." These parents can't imagine any good parent not noticing those kinds of things.

Seasoned parents insist that none of their children be sent home from school unless they have lost a great deal of blood or are unconscious.

First-timers look the teacher over with a clinical eye, uneasy about relinquishing parental right for 2 1/2 hours. Seasoned parents give the new teacher a solid pat on the back and say, "Good luck."

After the kids have finally been tucked into school for the year, the annual Back to School Night comes around. This is an evening set aside for parents to go to their children's schools and meet their teachers.

The regular agenda usually consists of a large gathering in the lunchroom, where PTA presidencies, principals, and teachers introduce themselves. Just in case any of the parents start getting bored and dozing off, the school nurse is often called in to keep this meeting interesting. School nurses like to talk about nice things like head lice. School nurses like to keep everyone calm by telling them how many cases of head lice they've detected in the school so far this year. They reassure nervous mothers that it doesn't matter how clean they are because head lice do not respect cleanliness.

About the time the nurse gets through with her relaxing part of the program, the principal excuses all parents for a short visit in the children's classrooms. Parents wander around for a while until they reach the right room.

Parents usually make a ritual out of trying to find their child's desk. If the desks aren't labeled, parents usually have their own private way of sniffing out their child's sitting quarters.

Sitting in a child's chair is not as easy as it may seem, especially in elementary school. Six-foot fathers have trouble keeping their knees from hitting their chins. Teachers usually give a well-prepared speech next, informing parents about the curriculum and the discipline for the coming year.

Maybe it has something to do with those little chairs, but something happens to every parent at about this point. Your knees may be up around your ears, but suddenly you're transported back to school again amid all the familiar school things . . . the green chalkboard with sample alphabet above, the pencil sharpener still smelling of shaved wood, wax crayons lined up in neat rows in yellow boxes, books covered with dirty fingerprints.

Parents remember the bully at recess, the "pigs-in-a-blanket" for lunch, and the time they threw up in the hall. They remember the spelling tests, the math tests, and the time they couldn't get to the bathroom in time.

Right about now parents want to grab their children, hug them, and say, "Hey, I remember. I was here once." But children aren't allowed to come to Back to School Night, so parents keep their hugs to themselves.

When the teacher finishes the speech, it's time for hand shaking. Parents search for something nice to say, and teachers search for something nice to say. Then parents start home with that hug still inside them.

The walk down the hall to the outside door is slower. Parents look the school over with their child's eyes. The walls stretch higher and the hall expands forever.

Children can't figure out why their parents hug them when they get home from Back to School Night. Parents don't understand it completely either. But it has to do with the realization that life can be difficult at any age.

And sometimes it's pretty tough out there.

Kids Really Know
How to Live

Efficiency, organization, and productivity are popular topics these days. Skim through the BYU Education Week catalogue and you'll see such topics as "Planning Your Life," "Time Management," "The Productive Pyramid," "A Lifetime of Excellence," and "How to Increase Your Self-Motivation." Walk through a local bookstore and you'll see best-selling titles like *How to Get Control of Your Time and Your Life.* Go to a Relief Society work night and you'll hear a lecture on "Life Management."

Everywhere I go, someone is telling me it is not enough to be busy. I need to be productive, organized, and efficient as well. I heard one dedicated life management lecturer say she didn't even go from one room of her house to another without her daily time planner.

I think there's a lot to say for being a slouch. My kids are great at being regular unorganized mess-pots, and they're happy.

I went to a funeral years ago, where a tribute was given to the deceased woman. "She had the cleanest windows in town," the speaker boasted. "She woke up early every morning and washed every window in her house."

Heaven help me if the only nice thing people can remember about me when I'm six feet under is how spotless my kitchen floor was. I want my children to remember me without a vacuum, mop, or toilet brush welded to my hand.

I took the children to the park one autumn day. While they played on the equipment, I tried to jog around the park efficiently, productively, and in an organized fashion. I managed to make hard work out of exercise.

My children didn't try to make what they were doing worthwhile. They hung by their knees on the monkey bars because they were tickled with the way the world looked upside down.

I thought about losing weight and getting my cardio-vascular system up to my training level. My children took a deep breath of the autumn-scented air and threw sand in each other's hair.

I want to reach back into myself and release the child. While I watched my children play, I learned something important about living. There is a place for efficiency and organization in everyone's life. But there is also an equally important place for spontaneity, unscheduled joy, and the simple healing balm of play.

Another thing kids have a knack for is honesty. Most adults admire this trait in a child. But I must admit, there have been times when I've found my children's flair for "telling it like it is" a little less than admirable.

Take the time my husband invited his boss home for supper. I had already given the children strict instructions not to throw food, put their feet on the table, or blow bubbles in their milk. Apparently I forgot one important don't.

Just as my husband's boss started to bring his first spoon-ful up to his mouth, my young son shouted across the table, "Hey! Do you want to know what those little black things are?" He pointed to the recessed light in our kitchen ceil-ing. "They're dead flies!"

Then there are the times when my two-year-old gets into mischief. She still allows her blessed honesty to come shining through as she approaches me with a sheepish frown and says, "Don't go look in your closet, Mom."

When I asked my four-year-old where he got the gum he was chewing, he thought carefully before he truthfully admitted to finding the gum on the sidewalk. "But don't worry, Mom," he reassured me. "I sucked off all the dirt before I ate it."

My children also insist on honesty from adults in their lives. When my two-year-old started coughing in a store the other day, she was approached by a kind, gentle older woman who said, "Oh, you have a little frog in your throat, dear. You wait here and I'll get you a little drink of water."

My four-year-old son quickly threw his arms out in front of the woman and defended his sister with, "My sister don't swallow frogs!"

My six-year-old daughter tugged on my sleeve while I was fixing dinner the other night. Apparently she was starting to doubt the wisdom of all this honesty business. "Do we have to tell the truth all the time?" she asked me.

I stopped working for a minute and tried to think of my first lesson in honesty.

"Why do you ask?" I said, stalling for time.

"Well, there's this boy in my class at school. His name is Jimmy. He sits at my table and well, he kinda, sorta, well, he . . . stinks. But I don't want to tell him, 'cause he's nice and sometimes he smiles at me. I'm afraid if I tell him, it would make him feel sad."

Ahh . . . kids. They soon catch on to our adult madness.

I remember when we introduced my daughter to her first Halloween trick-or-treat outing. When we got home, her mouth was wide open. "Mom," she said in amazement, "we went to houses and they gave me candy . . . all of them!"

She was no dummy. She knew a good thing when she found it. She tried trick-or-treating at least fourteen other times that year. When she came home one day in July with a sack full of candy, I didn't have the heart to tell her you only get to do that once a year.

Apparently my neighbors didn't, either.

More Than a
Macaroni Turkey

For most people, thoughts of Thanksgiving Day bring memories of steaming golden turkeys and tart cranberry sauce in Grandma's crystal bowl. And there are crowds of people wandering through those memories too: uncles with whiskers and bad breath who want to kiss you, brothers and sisters capping their teeth with black olives and blowing bubbles in their fruit punch. But each year when Thanksgiving Day approaches, I always turn my thoughts to elevators, kidney beans, and my mother's eyes.

School was out for the Thanksgiving holiday, and I was hurrying home carrying a turkey I'd made from colored macaroni, spaghetti, dried yellow corn, smooth round lentils, and kidney beans. The crisp autumn air, I remember, felt cool on my cheeks as I passed the fields of dried cornstalks rustling in the wind.

I was particularly proud of this artistic creation. I had been working on this turkey for weeks at school, making sure each bean and macaroni was in exactly the right place.

When I walked in the front door, I noticed my mother in the kitchen. She was busy fixing her famous raspberry, orange peel, and cranberry Jell-O salad for the big dinner the next day.

My mother was an accomplished oil landscape artist, and I wanted to take after her. This crude turkey was not my first attempt to please her with my "art." I slammed the front door behind me and ran into the kitchen, pushing the turkey proudly toward her.

Then the phone rang. As my mother jumped up to grab it, my turkey slid out of my hands and fell on the floor. An older brother and sister ran into the room just as I bent over to retrieve the broken pieces and knocked me over while they fought with each other. The baby crawled in and tried to stuff a fallen bean into her nose just as two young sisters came into the room and tried to get my mother to look at their school work. My mother covered the mouthpiece on the phone and said, "Will you kids be quiet and get out of here!"

I struggled to pick up the last of the fallen beans as my mother pushed me out of the room along with the rest of the kids. I walked to the elevator in our hallway on my way downstairs to find the glue to fix my unappreciated masterpiece. (I know most houses don't have elevators, but this one did. A previous owner had had the elevator installed for medical reasons.) The string to pull the light on in the elevator was too high for me to reach. I called for someone to come and turn it on for me, but nobody came. Finally, I just walked into the elevator alone and closed the door.

Once inside the pitch-black elevator, I pushed the down button. After the elevator had started down, a loose bean fell off the turkey. I decided to go back upstairs where there was some light so I could pick up the fallen bean. Because it was dark, I didn't realize my foot had slid outside the elevator encasement. When the elevator floor and the upstairs floor came together, my foot was sandwiched between them. Suddenly feeling a terrible rush of pain, I screamed and pushed the down button before my foot was ripped in two.

The upstairs door soon opened, flooding light into the elevator. My mother was standing above me. Before I knew what was happening, she had me in her arms and was carrying me into the kitchen. She filled the sink with water and ice and put my mangled foot in it while she called the hospital and the doctor. Then she picked me up and hurriedly carried me out to the car.

With my head in her lap, I looked up into my mother's blue eyes as she started the motor. Her eyes were full of shock and grief . . . and something more. She tenderly cradled my head with her free hand as she sped to the hospital.

I was the middle child in a big family and was always trying to do something extra well so my mother would notice me. But as my mother drove me to the hospital, it suddenly occurred to me that she loved me very much. She cared deeply about me. She didn't love me because I made nice bean turkeys or because I was a budding artist. She loved me just because I was me.

Somehow that knowledge seemed to flood my whole body with a warmth that took away the pain.

I knew that later there would be other children for my mother to console, other phones to answer, but that didn't seem to matter now. At that moment, I knew that my mother loved me, that she had always loved me, and that she would always love me.

So every year as I sit around the table filled with food at Thanksgiving, the memory returns. I am once again a frightened little girl deep in my mother's lap, and I can still remember the feeling.

Take One Gripe,
Go to Bed, and Call
Me in the Morning

The other day I overheard a conversation between two women in the checkout line at a local department store. It was the classic "working woman vs. stay-at-home woman" scenario, with the usual clichés.

You've heard all the phrases before. First the stay-at-home woman says, "Well, I stayed home, and I loved every minute of it."

The working mother replies, "I have my Ph.D., three genius children, and a full professorship, and I have loved every minute of it."

We women have become so defensive about our choices that we've created a major problem for ourselves: we can't complain anymore.

In the past, the stay-at-home woman used to be able to complain about the crayon marks on the sofa, the broken toilet, and those funny little people who were swinging from the rafters calling her Mom. Now she has to "love every minute of it." If she complains about all this stay-at-home bliss, someone will promptly tell her a quick solution to all her problems.

If she takes the suggestions and plants her wool-pleated skirt on a chair behind a typewriter or terminal somewhere, they won't even let her complain about eyestrain or office stress anymore.

You see, if you can't handle your new superwoman,

working-mom image, someone will surely tell you the solution to all your problems: "Go home and bake bread!"

In our eagerness to defend our "turf of womanhood," whether in or out of the home, we've forgotten to allow ourselves what every sane woman needs: something to gripe about.

I think it's like holding in your stomach when you're out in public. You can only do it for so long before you have to take a deep breath and let it all bulge out. It's all this smiling and arguing about how much we love our lives that's getting to us.

I think we're afraid that if we admit we hate dirty diapers or office politics, it will be an admission that we've made the wrong choices with our lives. In order to stay healthy in all this madness, I think we need to plant our feet firmly on the ground and say, "I stayed home, and I didn't love every minute of it!" or "I went to work outside the home, and I didn't love every minute of it!"

It would be such a relief to admit that we're human and that all life's choices are difficult at times. It would be like taking off a new girdle: Suddenly everyone would see that we're not perfect—but we'd be a lot more comfortable.

I'd Like to Reach Out and Throttle the Telephone Solicitor

I have composed a letter for every woman out there who has to answer the phone at home.

Dear telephone solicitor:

I know we've never met before, but I'd like to drop you a line. I know we are strangers, and strangers seldom correspond. So why, may I ask, did you, a total stranger, interrupt me just as I got settled in the bathroom?

You did not tell me you were selling insurance. You told me I had been chosen for a special free gift. Then you took the next two hours to tell me about your insurance. In your last breath, you finally told me it would only take $59.95 for postage and handling to have my free gift mailed to me.

May I offer a word of advice? Most people are not going to be interested in your light bulbs, carpet cleaning specials, or your life if you interrupt them when they have just gotten settled in the bathroom. People might even get angry.

You may have noticed how the telephone companies

tell us to "reach out and touch someone." Boy, do I wish I could reach out and grab you by the throat.

I try to be kind. I usually respond to you with comments like, "I'm sorry. I'm not interested." You are seldom discouraged by such niceties. I know they must give all telephone solicitors, human or computer, a crash course in how *not* to take no for an answer. But what you don't realize is what I really want to say to you.

What I want to say is, "You idiot! Do you realize I had to grab the baby halfway through a diaper change to answer this machine? I thought you might be somebody important. But you are *you*. I don't like you. I don't want to talk to you. I would do something terrible to you if I knew where you were calling from."

Now, don't get me wrong. I'm all for advertising, free enterprise, and apple pie. I'm even the daughter of an advertising man. It's just that I'm your captive audience not by my choice, but yours.

Newspaper advertisements, I can take. I can read newspaper ads when I'm comfortable and the kids are finally in bed. I can take the newspaper to the bathroom with me. I can use newspaper ads to start fires and line bird cages.

Television advertisers are a little harder to warm up to. Yet, some of the advertisements are even more entertaining than the programs. And I know what I'm going to get when I turn on commercial television. The television just sits there and doesn't bother me unless I ask it to. It doesn't suddenly sound an alarm while I'm bathing the baby, insisting that I come and listen to an ad for pantyhose.

There's something about the telephone that makes me jump. I sort of assume that someone I know will be on the other end. I could be sick in bed with a terminal illness, but somehow I would find a way to crawl over and answer the telephone.

There's an element of trust built into the telephone. You cannot be trusted.

Someday I'm going to make a million by inventing a

telephone zapper. At the touch of a button, this zapper will send out an electrical shock to any telephone solicitor who abuses my right of privacy.

Sincerely,

Your friendly resident

WINTER

We come home in winter, home to bright, warm kitchens with curtains drawn against the dark outside. Rediscovered ovens steam with spiraling curves of hot cinnamon rolls bulging with plump raisins, spices, and sugar. Forgotten boxes of mismatched gloves, boots, crumpled hats, and hand-knit scarves are pulled from storage to become familiar friends once more. Children in flannel nightgowns curl up by heat vents on frosty mornings, their knees bent to their chins.

We finish plowing dried cornstalks into the cold earth and step inside. We finish raking the last leaves from under the maple tree and step inside.

We have not yet been tucked under a blanket of snow, but it is near. We feel it coming. We pull our jackets closer and step inside.

We come home in winter.

Lasts, Not Firsts

As a mother, I have often been admonished to remember the firsts with my children—the first tooth, the first Christmas, the first step, the first ride on a two-wheeler.

Firsts are easy to notice. They seem to say, "Remember me. I am important." So I have dutifully remembered and recorded my children's firsts. I've watched, photographed, and written about them growing from first tooth to first dentist appointment, from first step to first victory at a school relay race and from first word to first talk in church.

Now I find myself thinking more about the lasts.

After my first child was born, I honestly thought late-night feedings would never end. I felt like a walking zombie from lack of sleep. When the baby finally slept through until dawn, I was ecstatic. My husband and I even celebrated that historic day with three cheers and a chocolate milkshake.

With each child, the feedings late at night seemed to come and go a little faster. I wasn't so anxious to have it all end. I began to wonder when it would be the last time I would feel my newborn's soft skin against mine as I nursed her and drowsily watched her relax back to sleep, cradled in my arms.

Now I have no more late-night feedings.

There will be a last time when my little bursting boy runs through the house scattering trucks and mud. "This is the last time I'm going to tell you to clean up this mess!" I often hear myself shout. Then tomorrow it is the last time, and my little boy is a young man, too mature for trucks and mud.

After I had complained to a neighbor about the children's sticky, dirty fingerprints all over my lower walls, she replied, "Don't worry, they'll soon be sticky, dirty fingerprints all over your upper walls. Children do grow up, you know."

And they do. Children refuse to stay small. Lasts don't cry out to be remembered. We find ourselves wondering, "When did he quit throwing his pudgy arms around my neck and kissing me goodnight? When did she put her dolls away and start having her own babies instead?"

There is not nearly as much time as I thought. It flutters past us like a leaf in the wind, here one minute, then gone on the next breeze. Maybe if we would try to capture the joy in today, we would truly relish and rejoice in all of the firsts . . . and the lasts.

If You Keep Your Feet on the Ground, You Can't Get Your Pants On

I saw her there at church again Sunday. She is an elderly widow who lives in my neighborhood. She sat on the hard wooden bench with an air of dignity during the prelude music.

But I noticed something else in her eyes when she looked longingly at my young children. Her face seemed to take on new animation, and she smiled broadly.

I have often envied her sitting there, alone, with no one to mawl her, pull her hair, fight over who gets the sacrament first, spit-up on her shoulder, snag her nylons, or throw all the contents of her purse out into the aisle.

No one interrupts her meditation with, "Mom, I have to go REAL bad!" or "I want to go home," or "How come I only get to take one piece of bread?"

She sat on the bench behind us. When the baby started to cry, she extended her arm and placed a gentle finger on the bench next to his hand. It was a new curiosity and my baby curled his pudgy fingers around her thin, wrinkled index finger. It occurred to me that it may have been a long time since someone had touched this woman.

I had recently read that when a person is touched, the amount of hemoglobin in the blood increases significantly.

Hemoglobin is a part of the blood that carries vital supplies of oxygen to all the organs of the body — including the heart and brain. An increase of hemoglobin tones up the whole body, helps prevent disease, and speeds recovery from sickness.

I turned and smiled at her as she entertained my baby with her touch. I noticed her purse sitting on the bench beside her. It was open, and I saw several containers of prescription drugs.

I remembered my mother's expression, "Hugging lifts depression. It greases up the old body's immune system like a good oil change. Regular hugging, like oil changes, keeps the body fresh and makes it run smoother longer." I wondered if doctors ever gave prescriptions for touch: Administer one hug, five times a day.

After the church meeting was over, she winked at my children and turned to me. "Teach them to be silly, to laugh and be affectionate," she said with an earnest voice. "I taught mine to be talented, dignified, and proper. I was always telling them not to touch, not to get dirty, not to be too loud. Now they come home in their fine cars with their fine clothes and talk to me, but they don't touch me.

"It's funny, but I was always telling my children to be more serious. I told them they have to keep their feet on the ground. Now they are serious. They used to say, 'But Mom, with your feet firmly on the ground, you can't get your pants on.' "

I smiled, and she smiled. I wanted to laugh . . . to reach out and hug her. But I didn't.

I wish I had. She walked away from the church alone.

My Mother, My Friend

The room felt cold when I entered. The noise and clatter of hurrying nurses and interns, along with the chatter of hospital personnel, were abruptly muted as the heavy wooden door closed behind me. I walked quietly into the private, sterile room.

My mother was resting in a hospital bed, wearing a starched hospital gown, waiting for surgery. Her eyes opened when she heard the door close. She smiled when she saw my face.

"How much longer will it be?" I asked, walking toward her.

"An hour or so," my mother answered. "Your father has gone down to the cafeteria for lunch."

I noticed how silver Mother's hair had become. I felt uncomfortable, even nervous. Mother was an early riser, and I had seldom seen her in bed before. It seemed unnatural. The color in her face was gone. She looked tired.

I didn't want her to look tired. I didn't want her to be ill. Always before, she had been the comforter and I the comforted. Our roles seemed oddly jumbled at that moment.

When I was a child, my mother had always tried to get me to rub her feet when she was ill or tired. A good foot rub, she claimed, could melt away life's troubles and pain.

But I didn't like to rub people's feet. So when she would point her small foot in my direction, I'd suddenly become busy with something else. The few times she had been able to pin me down long enough, I would hurry through the whole rubdown and take the first chance to run. But becoming a mother had changed my attitude about quite a few things. My attitude toward foot rubs was one of the dramatic changes I noticed.

I sat down on the end of the hospital bed and pushed aside the blankets. I picked up my mother's small foot and laid it gently in my lap. It felt warm and smooth to the touch. Without being bribed, begged, or threatened, I started to rub my thumbs in a circular motion on the arch of her foot. I watched the tense muscles in her body relax slowly. Her eyes became droopy. A shaft of light from the window was resting on her face.

Memories started flooding back as I watched her there. I remembered seeing my mother decked in a grass skirt and shells, complete with a flower behind each ear, crashing through the living room door to perform a lively Hawaiian War Chant dance for her couch full of measle-covered children.

I remembered seeing her brush a few hasty but careful strokes of smooth oil paint on a rough canvas to finish a roaring ocean or a snow-capped mountain or an amber evening sky, between changing the twins' diapers. The home I grew up in had a floor full of children and walls full of Mother's paintings.

I remembered seeing her on her hands and knees, gently padding a corner in her closet for a pregnant stray cat's nesting place, when she was pregnant herself. When my father questioned her wisdom in providing silk-cushion treatment for every stray pregnant cat in town, all she did was smile and pat her own protruding stomach. Then Dad would grin and bear it through another batch of soft, puff-ball kittens among his shoes.

I remembered the day she sent me to the bathroom to scrub the sink. When I had worked for a while and came back declaring the sink had a stain that just wouldn't come out, she sent me back a second time with instructions to use a little "elbow grease." After a long, futile search in the bathroom cupboards, I came back and told her I couldn't find any. She laughed as she put her arms around me and told me the meaning of the phrase.

I've never forgotten those two words, and when something in my life seems a little too hard to handle the first time around, I find myself going back a second time with a little "elbow grease."

Just then, a nurse opened the door and peered into the room. "We'll be ready for you in about twenty minutes, Mrs. Wolsey," she said.

Her interruption brought me quickly back into the present. I looked down at my mother's small foot and pulled the short, squared-off toes apart. Then I started tapping the ends of the toes. That was Mother's favorite part.

I looked up at my mother. Her soft blue eyes smiled back at me. No words were exchanged. But at that moment, all the roles seemed to crumble around me. I was no longer just the child and she only the mother. We were good friends and the most comfortable of companions.

I placed my mother's foot back on the bed and picked up the other one. "Hold on to your sheets, Mom," I said. "I'm going to use a little elbow grease on this one."

Life Has Room for Dreams to Grow

I know a couple who are celebrating their forty-fifth wedding anniversary today. You may know them too. They're the couple who live across the street and down two doors.

Forty-five years ago, they were young. They had big dreams. LaVern was going to be a famous novelist and tell all the important untold stories. Edna was going to be a portrait artist of world renown. They were going to have their dream house, a two-story white frame nestled in the privacy of oak and pine.

But LaVern was in school, and Edna soon became pregnant.

Years followed with tiny, cramped apartments, tuition to pay, and diapers to wash. And Edna was pregnant again.

After graduation, LaVern found a job teaching English at the local junior college and Edna was pregnant again.

He told funny stories to the children. She crayoned pictures with the children on the kitchen table. They saved for a down payment.

Their first home was not a two-story white frame nestled in aging pines and oaks. It was a small, one-level frame, and there was no landscaping at all. They planted trees and fixed and painted. And Edna was pregnant again.

He wished he could find time to write in his journal. She wished she could find time to paint portraits of her children because they were growing up and changing so fast.

With their family population explosion, LaVern decided he'd better add onto the house. He spent his workday hours teaching students to write novels. She spent her workday hours scrubbing her children's portraits off the living room walls.

Then there were recitals and school plays, football games and proms, worn-out station wagons and bathrooms. Before long there were graduations, weddings, and grandchildren.

Now LaVern is ready to retire and Edna has all the children married off. "Maybe now, I'll have time to write," he says. "But it will just have to wait until we get back from our trip to see Jamie get baptized, and Edna and I have always talked about going on a mission together."

"Maybe now I'll have time to paint," she says. "But it will have to wait until I get the peaches put up and my mini-lesson prepared, and put in a couple of sessions at the temple."

Now they are on their way home to spend a quiet evening together for their anniversary. They are holding hands as they walk up the sidewalk to their home.

When they look up, it seems to them that they are seeing their old home for the first time. The addition he built has made the house into a two-story. The trees they planted long ago are tall and aging.

There is a banner across the front porch saying, "Happy Anniversary Mom and Dad," in big bright red letters on butcher paper. Their children and grandchildren greet them when they step inside the door.

As LaVern and Edna watch their loved ones crowd around them, LaVern suddenly realizes he was the author who began each of his children's life stories. Edna suddenly realizes the children are her greatest masterpieces.

LaVern and Edna are sixty-five years young. He's still writing his life's story, and she's still completing her masterpiece, in their two-story, white frame house nestled in the privacy of oak and pine.

We Need Each Other

I went to the store to buy red flannel for the baby's Christmas stocking. Instead, I found the mother of an old high school friend. I told her to say hello to her daughter for me. She said her daughter wouldn't remember me. She said her daughter doesn't remember much these days; she's been undergoing psychotherapy for years now.

Dear friend, because you've gone away within yourself, may I write to you today?

I remember the first time I saw you. You were sitting quietly alone on a wooden bench at church. It was my first week there, and I was feeling lonely too. I noticed you looked and spoke a little differently from the other girls our age in the Laurel class. But I also noticed your eyes. They were soft and inviting.

The other girls told me you were mentally retarded. I know you knew how they laughed at you and told jokes about you behind your back, but you never did anything cruel in return. You simply smiled.

Once when I sat next to you at church, an old man came up to me later and told me that was the first time anyone had ever sat next to you. You had lived your whole life like this in this place.

We became friends, remember? I was the president of the Laurel class, and you were one of my counselors. But then I was always pretty busy, wasn't I?

I was a little too busy for you and other important things. I was busy going to the dances you were never invited to, marching in pep clubs you were left out of, and making the new friends you never had.

I'll never forget the day I saw you on the BYU campus years after our high school graduation. You beamed when you saw me and threw your arms around me. You had just received a nursing certificate, and you were soon to be married. Your eyes told me that, at long last, you were able to show those other girls and the whole world that they were wrong. You were somebody and you had something to offer. I thought it was so like you to choose a field where you could care for the sick and people in need.

Now your mother tells me that you've been through the depths of a terribly abusive marriage. She told me you broke under the pressure and were in a suicidal state. She said you had had a nervous breakdown. She told me that, mercifully, you don't remember much now.

It's been more than ten years since I saw you last. I've thought of you often throughout these years. But I always pictured you happily married, with a loving husband, children, and part-time work at the hospital. I didn't know you were in hell.

I don't know why things turned out the way they did for you. Now you're gone away to a place where I can't find you and talk to you. I weep for you, but you don't know I'm here. I loved you then and I love you now—but it wasn't and isn't enough. I hope someday you will come back and give me a second chance.

A long time ago you wrote a few simple words in my yearbook. The words were crowded into a corner of a page and written in small, hesitant script. They read: "Dear Janene: Thank you for being my friend."

I didn't do enough. No one did enough. We don't deserve you.

Dear friend, don't stay away too long. You see, now we need you more than you need us.

Death Before Life

The contractions began after midnight. The bleeding was profuse. I buried my face in my husband's chest as he quickly carried me to the car, then sped to the hospital.

The night was hot and black. The next contraction was intense and gripping. I felt as though I was being drawn down a deep pit with nothing to cling to. Then, as suddenly as it had begun, the rush of pain ceased. I drew a long, deep breath, preparing for the next contraction, as my husband sped up to the hospital entrance.

It was too early. Our Christmas baby wasn't due to be born for another five months.

My husband stopped the car. Racing around to my door, he quickly took me in his arms and hurried inside, where a nurse directed him to a small, sterile room.

With previous births, my husband had been at my side perspiring, one hand pressing against the painful place in my lower back, his quiet voice encouraging me through the difficult labor of birth. "Come on now, Jan," I remembered him saying. "You're doing great. You can do it." But now, my husband was a silent observer in the corner as a hurried nurse and doctor quickly took over in the emergency room.

Later, after the bleeding had slowed, the doctor told me to be philosophic as he flipped off his sterile gloves.

I was confused. "Where's my baby?" I asked. "I want to see my baby."

"You wouldn't want to see this," the doctor said as he handed the nurse a covered stainless steel tray.

The realization came slowly that our baby was dead. I

didn't want to believe it. Just that afternoon, I had been working on a baby quilt. I felt numb.

At the end of previous pregnancies, I had been pushed to the hospital exit in a wheelchair, my arms cradling a soft, flannel-wrapped newborn. That hot July night, I walked slowly out of the hospital with empty arms. I felt as though I had been robbed.

The doctor told me statistics say most women in their childbearing years will have a miscarriage or two. But statistics didn't take away my pain and sadness.

Back home, well-meaning friends and family told me to be glad the baby didn't live, because it would have been deformed. Others told me not to feel bad because I could always have another one. I felt my grief was dismissed by those around me, yet I felt an intense, overwhelming feeling of loss. My arms ached to hold my baby. I felt phantom kicks and often thought I heard a baby crying in the distance. I felt vulnerable and afraid I might lose another child, or my husband. My four-month pregnancy had brought four months of planning for the future. When our baby died, that future died.

What followed were months of anger, guilt, and depression, yet everyone seemed to tell me I had no reason to grieve. Society seemed to allow parents a month or two to grieve after the death of a newborn. Parents of stillborns were allowed even less, while those of us who had miscarriages were too often dismissed altogether.

Parents who have children die after showing signs of life are given eternal assurances. Latter-day Saint couples who have children die before birth are left with many unanswered questions. It has been Church policy not to perform temple ordinances for stillborn children, although they can be listed on family group sheets.

"When you had the miscarriage I felt tired and empty inside," my husband said. "Later, my concerns were for you and your pain. You were so tired and emotionally drained. I didn't know what to do to help you through the experience.

"Friends and family didn't expect me to grieve. I guess they figured it was you who had carried the baby and went through the miscarriage. I had nothing to do with it. I felt like I was on the outside.

"But I felt the loss deeply. I kept wondering why it had happened. It was a tremendous letdown. I kept wondering about that empty space in our family and if there was a spirit involved.

"When I first found out you were pregnant, there was this sudden burst of expectation. We planned. It was like we had put up our Christmas calendar on the wall and started counting down the days. Then suddenly, halfway through the month, we got a notice that Christmas had been cancelled."

Such feelings are described as "closet grief" because friends, relatives, and neighbors often think parents should be able to get over this experience quickly and be happy again. But each parent who experiences a pregnancy loss needs to experience a grieving process that is natural, common, and necessary.

"I had six miscarriages in a row," Janet, a young mother struggling to begin her family, said. "To me, it was still a baby even if it was only an inch long. It hurts to lose a baby. Every time I lost a baby, my doctor would act like it was no big deal and just say to get pregnant again. I told him I'd lost six. He told me he had a patient who lost thirteen. I guess that was supposed to make me feel better. It didn't.

"Most people avoid you or say things that make you feel worse. Many will try to be authorities and tell you how long to wait before you try again. All I wanted was for someone to put their arms around me and tell me they were sorry it happened. I just wanted someone to be there and care."

Brenda, a young mother of two preschoolers, had two miscarriages at home. "After each miscarriage," she said, "I had to go to the hospital until the bleeding had slowed. They put me in a room right across the hall from the nursery. Watching the nurses bring the healthy, beautiful babies out to their mothers was torture. I wanted to die.

"After my miscarriages, I went into a real depression. I wanted to sleep all the time. I felt angry when I was near other pregnant women. My husband didn't show his emotions. I thought he didn't care."

"I think men generally ignore the issue among themselves," Brenda's husband later expressed. "Men usually don't say anything among themselves. I think most men figure it's not that big of a deal for them. It was their wife that went through it. But I found it was a big deal for me too. It would have helped me a lot if someone had acknowledged that an unfortunate thing had happened in my family. It would have helped so much for someone, especially a man, to acknowledge that it was hard for me too."

As time passed, Brenda and her husband found themselves better able to accept what had happened. "After my depression lifted," Brenda said, "I felt like I could go through almost anything. I had felt alone and forsaken. But I had to come to a peace with it. God didn't cause it to happen, and neither did I. I know I have grown because of it. If something happened to my older children now, I think I could cope with it better."

Grief, though so individual, seems to follow a pattern of stages. These may overlap—my husband and I often found ourselves in different phases at different times. Each parent will be unique in going through the four stages of grief. But just knowing about them can help a great deal.

The first stage is shock and numbness. This happened to us initially and lasted from a couple of days to a couple of weeks. We learned that it is a normal, healthy defense. Our emotions at this time were often uncontrollable, and we sometimes had difficulty taking in information. Friends and family accepted our grief for a short time but did not understand that it takes a long time to resolve.

The second stage brings searching and yearning. We found ourselves looking for what was lost. If we had been able to see, touch, or take a picture of our baby, it might have helped at this stage. We often felt anger at our doctor and the nurses, and questioned why this had to happen.

The third stage brings disorientation and disorganization. This is most severe in the fourth and sixth months after the loss. Depression hits hardest at this time. We found ourselves wavering between lack of motivation and wanting to work all the time. We felt like overeating at times; other times we didn't want to eat at all. We found it difficult to make decisions. I often avoided going out of the house or to family gatherings.

The fourth stage brings acceptance. It took time and patience, but eventually our actions were no longer mechanical, and we were able to enjoy life and have a good time without feeling guilty.

While I was grieving, I found great assurances in the words of the Savior. He not only knew of my grief, but had carried it for me. "He is despised and rejected of men; a man of sorrows, and acquainted with grief. . . . Surely he has borne our griefs and carried our sorrows."(Mosiah 14:3-4.)

On one of my blackest days, I read these words of the Savior: "I will not leave you comfortless: I will come to you."(John 14:18.) "Peace I leave with you, my peace I give unto you: not as the world giveth, give I unto you. Let not your heart be troubled, neither let it be afraid." (John 14:27.)

After six miscarriages in a row, Janet had a baby boy. "I decided it was all worth it when we finally got our little boy," Janet said. "We named him Matthew because that name means 'gift from God.' "

It's been nine years since that dark July night when we lost our child. We now have six living children. And although my heart still aches each Christmas for our child who might have been born, I find quiet peace in the babe who was born on Christmas day, the light and life of this world. I don't have all the answers, but I have the peace of a child, the peace that someday I will know and understand, the peace that only the Savior can give. And so, I am content.

Now when I walk through the great, towering forests of our planet, I hear those gentle words from the Doctrine and Covenants that describe the nature of life during the Millennium: "And there shall be no sorrow because there is no death. And in that day, an infant shall not die until he is old; and his life shall be as the age of a tree." (D&C 101:29-30.)

To say that coping with a stillbirth or miscarriage means forgetting would be to try to diminish a very real sorrow. Maybe coping with this loss doesn't mean forgetting or even having the sorrow lessen with time. But maybe coping with this sadness means living with it . . . living more gently and fully, allowing this sadness to make the bearer a more Christlike person.

The realization of our limited mortality can make our stay here on earth more sweet and meaningful. I've learned that sorrow can harden or soften us, embitter us or cause us to see more appreciatively, limit our views or widen our horizons.

Seasons offer the rebirth of spring after the death of winter. As I observe nature around me, I realize life is a process of living, dying, and living again. The whole earth proclaims the miracle of the resurrection. I find great peace in the knowledge that my family is part of that great plan.

A Mother's Letter
to Her Unborn
Child

Dear Child,

It's been only a day since I lost you. Yesterday I had such plans for you and now today you are gone and where you are I cannot go.

You were the answer to your parents' prayers. You should have seen the look in your father's eyes when I told him you were coming. We were so happy. We told everyone you were on your way.

Each morning when I woke, I would stroke my palm across the place where you were growing. Your father teased me about wearing maternity clothes before I really needed to. But I wanted the whole world to know. Even morning sickness reassured me of your presence.

Whenever I went somewhere, I knew you were with me. It made me complete. I could never get over the miracle that somehow God and your father and I had created a human life.

Then I lost you.

I'll never forget you. You are my child. You have been part of me. But I miss you, and when I go out now, I feel alone. I don't see life in the same way since I lost you. I walk softer now. Life is more fragile, more precious.

I hope someday I will be able to have another baby. But it will never be the same as it was with you. The feelings I've had with you are separate and unique. I do thank God for the time we had together.

I love you. I may never be able to hold you in my arms, but I will always hold you in my heart.

Your Mother

A Father's Letter to His Unborn Child

Dear Child,

Last night I took your mother to the hospital. She was in so much pain. I wanted to stop what was happening, but I couldn't.

We had waited so long for you to come. When I found out you were on your way, I wanted to stop people on the street and tell them the good news. I took all the guys at my office out to lunch the day your mother told me.

I used to call your mother every day to find out how she was feeling. She always laughed and said she was fine. Sometimes during my lunch break at work, I would walk through the toy department of a store near my office. My life seemed to count for more. I felt like someone important. I was going to be someone's father. We put your crib on lay-away.

I don't understand why this had to happen. Our house is too big and too quiet. I have so many questions.

I didn't carry you inside of me, but you were part of me. Whenever I took your mother in my arms, you were there too.

It's hard to say good-bye when I never had the chance to say hello.

Your Father

Small Shadows, Large Memories

The Spanish Fork Cemetery is on a hill in the south part of town. A canyon breeze blows down through the century-old cedars that mark straight rows between the water-stained headstones. Some of the large, ornate grave monuments make long shadows when the sun sets in the evening sky. Small markers leave small shadows, but large memories.

When I walk along the road that winds around the north side of the cemetery, I always look for one small marker. I don't remember where it is now, but I can't forget John and Carolyn Swenson.

It's been years, but the memory is as clear as the air was that morning. My husband and I were standing silently at the graveside with a few other family members and friends when the limousine drove up.

When the funeral-home operator opened the long car door, we could see John and Carolyn inside. John was gently cradling the tiny coffin on his lap. Carolyn, only a few days from a hard delivery and birth, sat motionless, her face white and still, her eyes red and tired.

This was their first child, a son. His body had not been made to live more than a few days. John and Carolyn were young, newly married, two gentle, quiet, sensitive people we had known in high school. They had waited a long time for this baby.

We had lost contact the past few years. We, like them,

were busy trying to get through school. Then we heard about their baby.

It was a simple graveside service. Carolyn's arms reached out, then drew back as John leaned over to place the tiny coffin in the earth. The wind was cold. John slipped his arm around Carolyn and they clung to each other, so tightly their knuckles went white.

Together, they quietly and graciously acknowledged each condolence, reserving their grief for solitude. I couldn't think of the right words as we stood with them that morning. I can't think of the right words today.

Months later, John and Carolyn surprised us with a visit on Christmas morning. Our young children had made a giant mess of wrapping paper and toys all over the living room floor. I kept apologizing for the mess and the silly antics of my children as they vied for John and Carolyn's attention.

Carolyn said, "Please don't apologize." She looked at my children, took a deep breath, and smiled. Then I understood.

John helped the children build a tower with their new blocks. Carolyn rocked my baby.

Ultrasound

She had always thought of machines as the modern way of losing the human touch—cold, impersonal, mechanical monsters.

After four long months of anxiety and repeated disappointing attempts to locate a heartbeat from the child she was carrying, there seemed little hope. An ultrasound test was ordered.

Cold and alone she sat on the examination table in a sterile hospital gown. She knew that in a few moments someone would be telling her of life or death. Though she longed to know, she now suddenly didn't mind if the doctor took his time getting to her room.

"Hello," a strange man said, walking into her room. "I'm Dr. Williams." He proceeded to push numerous buttons on one of the machines that surrounded her.

She lay down at his instruction and waited while he applied a sticky gel to her abdomen. He pushed a few more buttons and then ran an instrument over the gel.

Suddenly, there was movement on the screen of the machine beside her bed. In black and white, she saw a tiny, complete human being, stretching and crossing its legs, reaching its arms over its head, and rolling over and back. There was a clearly visible heart beating and pulsating within the child . . . her child.

The machine also showed the placenta and how it had implanted on the upper front portion of the uterus, temporarily blocking out fetal heart tones and cushioning movement. But that was of no medical concern.

A few touches on a few buttons, a little gel, and life or death can be pronounced.

Later she was handed the first snapshot of her newest child, a tiny, seventeen-week-old fetus who is very much alive.

Bethlehem by Bus

Years ago I made a pilgrimage to Bethlehem by bus. Instead of a quiet stable, I found an ornamented golden altar and souvenir shops. Instead of a heavenly choir, I heard the voice of a pushy salesman saying, "You buy souvenir, yes? Very cheap!"

Instead of a humble family, I found tourists, money changers, and merchants. I had imagined a much different Bethlehem. The contrast was disappointing.

There is an olive-wood, hand-carved Nativity set on top of my piano that reminds me of that visit. It also reminds me of something else.

Now my own small children finger the figures of wood and act out the Christmas drama in mismatched pajamas. As I watch them, I realize it is not the place but the event that is important. And the event, the physical part of it as well, is more real to me. Having given birth, I feel a special sort of kinship with Mary. I rode in a heated car to a sanitary hospital. Mary rode a donkey to a crowded stable.

When I hold the figure of Mary in my hands now, I wonder how things went for her . . . how much pain she was in, how tired and sore she must have felt that night. I contemplate the divine Sonship of her child.

I wonder how Joseph felt, too. I wonder if he was as nervous as my husband was during our first child's birth. I wonder if he held her hand, if he rubbed her back. I wonder if anyone was with them, or if they faced this event alone — together.

As I hold the tiny wooden baby Jesus in my hands, I

wonder, "Did they know? Did they know that someday this child would reign as king?" It makes me look at my own children with more reverence and ask myself, "Who are you? Who will you become?"

My thoughts often drift back to Bethlehem during the Christmas season. But I know my holy city will be wherever in the world I live, if only I live as Christ lived. I don't have to return to Bethlehem to experience the significance of the event that took place there.

Now my pilgrimage is not to Bethlehem by bus. My pilgrimage is home to my family and the hope each of my children offers to the world.

Grandma's Shopping List

If you are one of those grandparents who gets all confused and frazzled at Christmastime, let me offer a last-minute gift guide for your grandchildren that is sure to calm your nerves.

Most suggestions for shoppers at this time of year give ideas for toys that are educationally appropriate for your grandchild's age level. But there are a few things these suggestions don't tell you.

If your grandchild is a year or younger, you're free and clear. Your grandchild doesn't know what Christmas is. Your infant granddaughter doesn't know how to say, "Me want computer." She's still working on "Grandma." This is the best billing you'll ever have. Wrap up yourself. Baby will be thrilled.

Now, if you have a hard time controlling your urge to run out and buy that expensive crib mobile, stuffed worm that glows in the dark, or designer diapers, what you'll find is this: Come Christmas morning, your grandchild will promptly throw away the present and suck on all that great noisy bright wrapping paper. If baby is slightly older than a year, he will throw away the toy *and* the wrapping and opt to play with the box it came in.

If your grandchild is two years old, the most important question to ask yourself at the toy store is, "Can this thing be flushed down the toilet?" If the answer is yes, don't even consider buying it. Buy your grandchild a case of beets and tell him not to touch it. He'll love them.

The next important question to ask yourself is, "Does this thing have many small parts?" People who make toys with small parts hate parents. The only things small parts are good for are choking on, losing, dropping down heat vent ducts, scattering, and, of course, flushing down the toilet.

Make sure to color-coordinate your two-year-old's goodies with his clothes. That way the stains won't show as much.

If your grandchild is three years old, ask yourself this question before you even take a toy off the shelf to look at it, "Will this thing survive if it is stepped on, thrown across the room, flushed down the toilet, or smashed against little brother's head?" Or perhaps an even more pertinent question would be, "Will little brother survive if this thing is smashed against his head?"

If your grandchild is four, refrain from the urge to buy clothing. I know it is so marvelous to finally dress your grandchild without the diaper bulge, and your son or daughter deserves a medal for making it through toilet training, but don't get carried away and do something foolish. Four-year-olds regularly grow two inches the night before they try on new clothes in the morning. And if by chance you actually buy something that fits, it will be too itchy, stiff, dressy, plain, or the wrong color. Four-year-old children like to dress themselves in pants with holes in the knees, shirts that don't match, socks with "bumps" on the toes, and shoes with laces that zap undone every time you take your eye off them.

If your grandchild is five, ask yourself, "Will this thing become useless after it is dragged through snow, scraped across sidewalks, and plopped in mud puddles for six blocks?" In other words, can your grandchild safely take it to kindergarten for show and tell?

The other question to ask before buying your five-year-old a gift is, "How much trade-in or exchange value does this thing have?" Kids in kindergarten love to trade or exchange things like coats and hats when there is a head lice scare or chicken pox when it's going around.

So take a deep breath and relax. One of the nicest things about having grandchildren is that it gives you a good excuse for spending long hours in the toy department buying all the things you wanted as a kid. Who says you have to actually give them to the grandchildren?

No Peace on Earth During Our Rehearsals

The other day, I overheard the children casting themselves for our annual ad lib Christmas pageant. Every year on Christmas Eve, my husband and I gather our young children around us and read the Christmas story from the Bible.

What started as a spontaneous plea from the children to let them act out the story has now become a tradition. Now, preparations for the pageant start a little earlier.

"I get to be Mary," I heard April, our seven-year-old, dictate to her four younger brothers and sisters.

Aubrey, our six-year-old, was quiet for a few minutes. I knew she wanted to be Mary too, but her years have taught her a simple truth: firstborn children usually get to do what they want to do . . . first. Aubrey was born second. She thoughtfully rechose her role.

"I guess I'll be the shepherd," she said quietly.

"No! I want to be the shepherd!" Jordan, our four-year-old, insisted.

"You have to be Joseph," Aubrey answered, " 'cause you're a boy."

"I don't want to be Joseph," Jordan said, standing his ground. "Joseph's just our baby."

"No, I mean Joseph, Mary's husband," Aubrey said. "Joseph is going to be baby Jesus." (Joseph is our nine-month-old baby boy, so things are getting a bit confusing here.)

"Me, Baby Jesus," our two-year-old daughter, Arianne, piped up. She never likes to miss a good fight.

"No, Annie," Aubrey answered. "You too big. Joseph has to be baby Jesus."

"All right," April said, taking charge of the situation. "Joseph is baby Jesus. Annie, you be the donkey. No, wait—we need a bigger donkey. Dad, he'll be the donkey. Annie, you're the lambie. Jordan, you're Joseph. Aubrey, you can be the shepherd. Mom can be the angel, 'cause she doesn't have to step on a chair to get her face up in the sky."

Then I heard April run and grab a blanket to wrap the baby in for a dress rehearsal. Jordan wrapped a bathroom towel around his head and found the yardstick for his staff. Aubrey taped cotton balls to Arianne's underpants for the lamb's tail.

I peeked from the kitchen door just in time to see Mary and Joseph lovingly laying baby Jesus in a cardboard box. The shepherd led her little lamb to the couch.

"Hark!" the shepherd dramatically announced. Then she jumped off the couch and ran to the kitchen door to give me my cue. "Mom, you're Herald," she whispered into the kitchen. "When I say your name, sing." Then she ran back to the couch. "Hark, the HERALD angel sing," she said, pointing to me for my entrance.

Just as I stepped into the dress rehearsal from the kitchen, baby Jesus pulled himself to a standing position in the cardboard box, then tumbled headfirst to the floor. Joseph hit Mary on the head with his staff, and the lamb started plucking off her cotton-ball tail and stuffing it into her nose.

"Glory to God in the highest," I sang in my best alto voice, then, a little more quietly, "and peace on earth, goodwill toward men."

I wonder if Mary ever had moments like these.

Our family debut on the Christmas sacrament meeting

program didn't go any better. We had been practicing for weeks. We thought the children were totally prepared.

When it came time for our family to sing, we marched up to the front and I sat quietly down at the piano, ready to start the introduction. My husband arranged our children in an orderly fashion in front of the microphone. He placed the two-year-old and the four-year-old in front, arranged the other children behind them, and held the baby in his arms.

Everyone smiled. The older ladies in the congregation nodded in slumber.

Then I began the introduction to our family Christmas song. When the children were supposed to start sweetly singing, our two-year-old grabbed the microphone and sucked the entire thing into his mouth. Then he let out a foghorn yell so loud that all those older ladies suddenly weren't dozing anymore.

This two-year-old loved his newfound power. He noticed that if he made funny sounds when he had this metal object in his mouth, all the people in the audience would pop up and their eyes would bulge out.

My husband had to set the baby down in order to grab the two-year-old. The two-year-old didn't want to be grabbed and have his new toy taken away. He immediately began pounding my husband over the head with his fists in protest while the baby, just set free, ran over to me at the piano and began pounding on the keys. By this time the four-, six-, and eight-year-olds got the giggles and were at a complete loss for their singing voices. The nine-year-old was totally embarrassed with her whole family. Someone from the audience ran up and distracted the baby from banging on the piano so I could start the introduction again.

Please don't ask me how the song went.

Confined, Yet Free

Blanche was an elderly lady who lived in my ward. We met over the telephone when my doctor sent me to bed because of premature labor. After three weeks, I was ready to climb the walls. But it had been three years for Blanche.

Bedridden for three years because of a stroke, Blanche had previously been confined to a wheelchair for thirty-four years. She was seventy now, and the effects of age added to her problems.

When she was in her early thirties, Blanche went into the hospital for simple surgery. The doctor made a tragic mistake, cut a nerve, and paralyzed her. She had four young children at the time. Her alcoholic husband left her when he found that she was paralyzed. That was thirty-seven years before I met her.

"At first I was upset," Blanche told me as we talked over the phone. "But I soon got over it. I couldn't just give up because I couldn't walk. I had a family to raise." She was too busy for bitterness.

"I must be here for a purpose," Blanche told me. "Now that I can't get into my wheelchair, I have to just keep plugging along. But I have so much to be grateful for. I count my blessings every day. Last weekend my granddaughter came by with her husband and her little baby. Little children are so precious, and they grow up so fast. You see, I have a lot to live for."

Blanche and I became good telephone friends during our mutual bedridden days. Whenever we talked, she would describe the view from her window to me. She observed and described in detail the beautiful changes that the sea-

129

sons brought to the tree outside her window. "I am so grateful I can see," she said, with a deeper reverence for nature and her gift of sight than I had ever known in a person.

Blanche and I were both confined, but as we became friends, I knew there was a difference. I would soon be set free. Blanche would remain. She never said it in so many words, but she taught me that no person or thing can really confine a person. In many ways, she was freer than I.

Our telephone conversations continued after my baby was finally born, healthy and beautiful. Blanche seemed as excited as I felt when I could finally get out of bed.

She often called after that to wish me a happy Thanksgiving or a merry Christmas or just to see how I was. She never let me know of her pain. I planned to visit her when I got over a lingering infection I had developed after the baby was born. I never got the chance.

Blanche died a few months after my baby was born. It was a cold, stormy, winter day when they held her funeral, but hundreds of people came. Hundreds of people had been touched by her attitude toward life. Hundreds of people found new courage to face their problems after seeing the way she faced hers.

Blanche was finally able to get out of bed. I like to picture her square dancing in heaven, a real foot-stomping, leg-slapping, down-home shindig.

Sometimes when I'm feeling a little trapped or a little blue, I wish I could call Blanche. I know she'd give me the most marvelous description of heaven. I know she would tell me I'm down here for a purpose, and to just keep plugging along and count my blessings.

In Conclusion

A middle-aged woman approached me after I had finished giving a talk to her Relief Society and asked, "I have
two children at home, two in elementary school, two in
junior high school, two in high school, one on a mission,
and one married with kids of her own. What does that
make me . . . a mother for all seasons?"

"Tired," I replied.